Nuclear Madness

What You Can Do!

With a new chapter on
Three Mile Island

Dr. Helen Caldicott

with the assistance of
Nancy Herrington & Nahum Stiskin

BANTAM BOOKS

TORONTO · NEW YORK · LONDON · SYDNEY

NUCLEAR MADNESS

*A Bantam Book / published by arrangement with
Autumn Press*

PRINTING HISTORY

Autumn Press edition published December 1978
2nd printing .... April 1979
3rd printing .... June 1979
4th printing .... December 1979
Excerpted in THE PROGRESSIVE, *December 1978; and* NEW AGE
Magazine, June 1978.

*A portion of this book appeared in "Accidents Will Happen:
The Case Against Nuclear Power" by Environmental Action
Foundation published by Harper & Row Publishers, Inc. 1979.*

Bantam edition / November 1980

ISBN 0–553–14606–8

Published simultaneously in the United States and Canada

Bantam Books are published by Bantam Books, Inc. Its trademark, consisting of the words "Bantam Books" and the por-
trayal of a bantam, is Registered in U.S. Patent and Trademark
Office and in other countries. Marca Registrada. Bantam
Books, Inc., 666 Fifth Avenue, New York, New York 10103.

PRINTED IN THE UNITED STATES OF AMERICA

0 9 8 7 6 5 4 3

A MESSAGE THAT MAY SAVE
ALL OUR LIVES

"An eloquent and accurate assessment of the nuclear threat: the arms race which threatens our survival."

—Richard Barnet, Coordinator,
Institute for Policy Studies

"Helen Caldicott's message—delivered with sound facts, sincere compassion, and irresistible conviction—needs to be heard now!

—John W. Gofman, M.D., Ph.D., Chairman,
Committee for Nuclear Responsibility

"Required reading for all members of the human race, particularly for those of us blessed with the political freedom to make choices on our future direction."

—Dale Bridenbaugh,
Nuclear Engineer

"An excellent account for the lay public about the imminent dangers of the nuclear age. It should be read by all voting members of an informed democracy."

—Thomas Najarian, M.D.

"At last, a book that should awaken America to the dangers of the nuclear age, combining the authority of an expert, the passion of a mother, and the vision of a world citizen."

—Richard Falk, Ph.D.,
Professor of International Law,
Princeton University

"This simple, passionate, yet reasonable book is must reading for all citizens. Dr. Caldicott is a well-educated pediatrician—and a brave person who is not afraid to speak her mind."

—Charles A. Janeway, M.D.

ABOUT THE AUTHOR

Australian-born and educated, DR. HELEN CALDICOTT practices pediatrics at Boston's Children's Hospital Medical Center. An environmental activist since 1971, she virtually single-handedly educated and inspired the Australian public to protest—and bring a halt to—French atmospheric testing in the South Pacific. She later worked tirelessly to inform Australia's labor unions about the medical and military dangers associated with the mining and sale of Australian uranium on the international market. Married and the mother of three children, Dr. Caldicott is now a permanent resident of the United States—where she is rapidly becoming a leading critic of the nuclear power and armaments industries. In *Nuclear Madness,* and in her frequent lectures and T.V. and radio appearances, she urges us all to become better informed about the nuclear hazards we face—and challenges us to take action to assure human survival on planet Earth.

To Bill,
to my children Philip, Penny, and William,
and to all the children of the world.

Acknowledgments

I gratefully acknowledge the helpful criticism given by Tom Adams, Mary Baker, Richard Barnet, Rosalie Bertell, Dale Bridenbaugh, William Davidon, Lester del Ray, Richard Falk, Daniel Ford, Randall Forsberg, Ann Freedgood, John Gofman, Dolph Honicker, Charles Janeway, and Thomas Najarian.

Table of Contents

Nuclear Threats to Human Survival

NUCLEAR WEAPONS
(Design, Testing, Production,
Storage, Deployment)

⬇ **UNDERGROUND EXPERIMENTS**

U **UNIVERSITY REACTORS**

⊘ · **MILITARY AND ERDA ('72) REACTORS
AND RESEARCH FACILITIES**
Accounting for 50% (appr.) of All Radioactive Waste

⌂ **NUCLEAR POWER PLANTS (Commercial)**
Accounting for 50% (appr.) of all Radioactive Waste

▲ **UNDER CONSTRUCTION**
▮ **OPERABLE**
● **PLANNED**

NUCLEAR INDUSTRIES

URANIUM MILL TAILINGS

TRANSPORTATION/STORAGE OF RADIOACTIVE MATERIALS

RADIOACTIVE WASTE BURIAL GROUNDS

Map prepared in 1972 by L. Franklin Ramirez, and designed by Mercedes Naveiro. Information from Another Mother for Peace. Commissioned by Women Strike for Peace.

1

Our Own Worst Enemy

I am a child of the Atomic Age. I was six years old when American atomic bombs were deployed against the Japanese, and I have grown up with the fear of imminent annihilation by nuclear holocaust. Over the years my fear has increased. Thousands of nuclear weapons are now being built each year. At this writing, 263 nuclear reactors are in operation in 22 countries around the world, 75 of them in the United States, licensed by the Nuclear Regulatory Commission. Two more are operated by the Department of Defense. 50,000 nuclear weapons exist on the planet. Nuclear technology stands to inherit the earth.

As a physician, I contend that the power and weapons industry nuclear technology threatens life on our planet with extinction. If present trends continue, the air we breathe, the food we eat, and the water we drink will soon be contaminated with enough radioactive pollutants to pose a potential health hazard far greater than any plague humanity has ever experienced. Unknowingly exposed to these radioactive poisons, some of us may be developing cancer right now. Others may be passing damaged genes, the basic chemical units which transmit hereditary characteristics, to future generations. And more of us will inevitably be affected unless we bring about a drastic reversal of our government's pronuclear policies.

I learned about the carcinogenic (cancer-causing) and mutagenic (gene-altering) effects of nuclear radiation during my first year of medical school, in 1956. At that time the United States and Russia were conducting atmospheric bomb tests. My genetics teacher did not connect his lectures on radiation to the fallout

1

produced by these explosions, but the relationship became clear to me when newspapers reported that radioactive strontium-90, a by-product of atomic testing, had been carried around the world by high-level winds, deposited on the earth as nuclear fallout, and was being found in high concentrations in cow's milk and in the deciduous teeth and, presumably, the bones of children. At the same time, the long-term medical consequences of radiation were just beginning to appear, in the form of an increased rate of leukemia among Japanese A-bomb survivors.

Most Americans with whom I've spoken know very little about the medical hazards posed by nuclear radiation and seem to have forgotten (or suppressed) the atomic-bomb anxiety that was so prevalent in the 1950s. Back then, most Americans were aware of the devastation that nuclear war implies: Children were constantly diving under their desks and crouching in school corridors during simulated nuclear attacks, while the bomb shelter business boomed and the nation prepared a program of civil defense. Americans were justifiably scared. People recognized that nuclear disarmament could mean the difference between a secure future for them and their children, and no future at all.

But during the 1960s the American public became preoccupied with other matters: political assassination, the Civil Rights movement, the Vietnam war. The threat of nuclear holocaust was submerged by these more immediate problems. Only the Pentagon sustained its interest in nuclear development: in the effort to keep ahead of the Soviet Union, America's military strategists continued to stockpile more and more atomic weapons, while developing and refining delivery systems, satellites, and submarines.

Today, however, it is of the utmost urgency that we refocus our attention on the problems posed by nuclear technology, for we have entered and are rapidly passing through a new phase of the Atomic Age. Despite the fact that reactor technology is beset with hazardous shortcomings that threaten the health and well-being of the nations that employ it, nuclear power plants are spreading throughout the world. Moreover, by making "peaceful" nuclear technology available to any nation wealthy enough to buy a nuclear reactor, we are inviting other countries to join the international "nuclear club" militarily, as well as economically. Following India's lead in 1974, many nations are bound to explode test devices in the coming years. Because of this proliferation of nuclear weapons, the likelihood of nuclear war, the most ominous threat to public health imaginable, becomes greater every day.

In view of the threat that nuclear technology poses to the ecosphere, we must acknowledge that Homo sapiens has reached an evolutionary turning point. Thousands of tons of radioactive materials, released by nuclear explosions and reactor spills, are now dispersing through the environment. Nonbiodegradable, and some potent virtually forever, these toxic nuclear materials will continue to accumulate, and eventually their effects on the biosphere and on human beings will be grave: many people will begin to develop and die of cancer; or their reproductive genes will mutate, resulting in an increased incidence of congenitally deformed and diseased offspring—not just in the next generation, but for the rest of time. An all-out nuclear war would kill millions of people and accelerate these biological hazards among the survivors: the earth would be poisoned and laid waste, rendered uninhabitable for aeons.

As a pediatrician, I have devoted most of my professional life to working with children born with cystic fibrosis, the most common inherited childhood disease. The abnormal gene that carries this fatal disorder is found in 1 in 20 Caucasians; the disease's incidence is 1 in 1,600 live births. Watching my patients die of respiratory failure, and seeing other children in the wards die of leukemia and cancer, has motivated me to speak publicly and write this book. Knowing that the incidence of congenital diseases and malignancies will increase in direct ratio to the radioactive contaminants polluting our planet, I cannot remain silent.

"But what can *I* do, as an individual?" is a refrain I hear whenever I draw people's attention to the problems threatening our survival. The international balance of terror, economic pressures, and the frustration of dealing with a biased government and unresponsive bureaucracy leave many Americans feeling helpless. Many seem to believe that it has simply become impossible for an individual to influence the course of national and world events.

I disagree. My experience in Australia from 1971 to 1976 taught me that democracy can still be made to work—that by exerting electoral pressure, an aroused citizenry can still move its government to the side of morality and common sense. In fact, the momentum for movement in this direction can only originate in the heart and mind of the individual citizen. Moreover, it takes only one person to initiate the process, and that person may be politically naive and inexperienced, just as I was when I first spoke out.

My personal commitment to human survival was sparked when I read Bertrand Russell's autobiography. In Russell I found the moving example of a man who faced up to the dangers of the Atomic Age and, despite all odds, dedicated himself to ridding the earth of nuclear weapons. By 1962 his "ban the bomb" movement had culminated in the International Atmospheric Test Ban Treaty signed by the United States, Great Britain, and the Soviet Union—and the world briefly waxed hopeful that the superpowers would begin to disarm. When, in 1971, I discovered that France had been conducting atmospheric tests over its small colony of Mururoa since 1966, contravening the treaty inspired by Russell's work, I became indignant. I knew that when an atomic bomb explodes near the earth's surface, the mushroom cloud that billows into the sky carries particles of radioactive dust. Blown from west to east by stratospheric winds, these particles descend to the earth in rainfall and work their way through soil and water into the food chain, eventually posing a serious threat to human life.

At the time few Australians knew of the testing or were aware of its inherent dangers. I decided that it was my duty, as a physician, to protest France's disregard for the health of my fellow Australians, and I began by writing a letter to a local newspaper. That letter generated some supportive correspondence, and a TV news program asked me to comment on the medical hazards posed by fallout. France had tested another nuclear device, and planned to detonate four more in the next few months. Each time the French tested a bomb, I appeared on television again, explaining the dangers of radiation. As the public became better informed, a movement to stop the French tests coalesced around the medical facts.

The informal campaign that grew up around these televised talks gained greater momentum when I exposed a secret government report, passed on to me by a sympathizer employed by the State Government of South Australia, which confirmed that in 1971 a high level of radiation had been found in South Australian drinking water: In June 1972 government inspectors detected 1,860 picocuries of radiation per liter of rainwater, compared with a normal background radiation level of 50 picocuries and the "safe" maximum of 1,000 arbitrarily established by the International Commission of Radiological Protection. Shocked by the realization that their water supplies were now sufficiently contaminated to pose a genuine threat to them and their children, the citizens of Australia took action. Thousands joined marches held in Adelaide, Melbourne, Brisbane, and Sydney; a spate of editorials and statements by eminent scientists demanded an end to the testing; newspapers devoted full pages to angry letters from readers; dockworkers refused to load French ships; postal workers refused to deliver French mail; consumers boycotted French products. A Gallup poll showed that within a year 75 percent of the Australian public had grown opposed to the French tests. And on June 15, 1972, in response to enormous public pressure, the Australian government instructed its representatives to the U.N.'s Stockholm Conference on the Environment to vote in favor of a resolution calling for an end to all nuclear testing.

Although the Australian government was beginning to shift its position in response to public demand, the French remained unmoved, and it was decided by the committee coordinating the groups working together to stop the French tests that a delegation of concerned citizens should fly to Tahiti to lodge a formal protest with the governor of France's South Sea islands. The group was to include churchmen, union representatives, and Dr. Jim Cairns, deputy leader of the Australian Labor Party. I was invited to go along. Moments before we were to depart, however, we learned that French officials in Tahiti had announced that our group would be denied the right to disembark. We then decided to go to Paris with our protest. Twenty-four hours later, Jim, Ken Newcombe (leader of the Union of Australian Students), and I arrived in London, where we addressed a large crowd of Australians and New Zealanders in Hyde Park and delivered a letter of protest to the French embassy. Unfortunately, Britain's Parliamentarians were far more concerned with securing England's entry into the Common Market than with hearing about the radioactive fallout then contaminating Australia, and Prime Minister Harold Wilson declined to meet with us. We were not surprised when we met with an equally cold political reception in Paris the next day. The bureaucrats with whom we exchanged opinions were closed to our arguments; they insisted France needed its own *force de frappe* and that it would under no circumstances yield to public pressure. Stubbornly claiming that their nuclear tests were harmless, these professional bureaucrats nevertheless conceded that they would never consider conducting such tests in the Mediterranean: "Mon Dieu, there are too many people there!" We returned to Australia feeling that we had presented our case as forcefully as we could, but sorely disappointed by the arrogant disdain with which we were received.

In November, however, the momentum began to shift dramatically in our favor: A conference of Pacific nations convened by Australia and New Zealand spearheaded a U.N. vote to outlaw nuclear testing. The French countered with an announcement that 1973 would bring a new series of tests, including a 1-megaton hydrogen bomb blast over Mururoa Atoll. One month later, an enraged Australian public elected the Australian Labor Party, which opposed the action of the French, into office. Calling for an injunction to compel the French to desist from further atmospheric testing in the Pacific, the newly elected Australian government, and the government of New Zealand, took France before the International Court of Justice in the Hague. Although the Court's decision was disappointingly equivocal, France finally backed down in the face of world opinion and announced that it would restrict its testing to underground sites.

In our struggle to put an end to atmospheric nuclear testing, we had demonstrated that one voice was all it took to raise a warning call, and that once enough other voices joined in, that call would be heard around the world.

My experience in the struggle I have just described, and in others in Australia and the United States, has taught me many things: first and perhaps most important, that we can no longer afford to entrust our lives, and the lives and health of future generations, to politicians, bureaucrats, "experts," or scientific specialists, because all too often their objectivity is compromised. Most government officials are shockingly uninformed about the medical implications of nuclear

7

power and atomic warfare, and yet they daily make life-and-death decisions in regard to these issues. Some responsibility for this ignorance rests with my medical colleagues: too many of us are reluctant to look beyond our research laboratories or hospital corridors, and too many of us have remained silent about the medical hazards of nuclear technology and the radiation it produces, despite the fact that we acknowledge such radiation to be a certain cause of cancer and genetic disease.

My experience also taught me that the survival of our species depends on each individual. The growing controversy surrounding nuclear fission is the most important issue that American society and the world at large has ever faced. A national and international debate on this subject is long overdue, and the participation of each individual will determine its outcome. We must begin today by first of all learning as much as we can about the critical health hazards involved, because what we don't know about these dangers may kill us:

- The world's major military powers have built tens of thousands of atomic bombs powerful enough to kill the world's inhabitants several times over.
- Each 1,000-megawatt nuclear reactor contains as much radioactive material ("fallout") as would be produced by one thousand Hiroshima-sized bombs. A "meltdown" (in which fissioning nuclear fuel and the steel and concrete structures that encase it overheat and melt) could release a reactor's radioactive contents into the atmosphere, killing 50,000 people or more and contaminating thousands of square miles.
- Each reactor daily leaks carcinogenic and mutagenic effluent. These radioactive materials enhance the level of background radiation to which we are constantly exposed, increasing our risk of developing cancer and genetic disease.
- Each reactor annually produces tons of radioactive waste, some of which remains dangerous

for more than 500,000 years. No permanent, fail-safe method of disposal or storage has yet been found for them, despite millions of dollars spent during three decades of research. Despite recent proposals, there is good reason to suspect that we may never develop safe methods of disposal and long-term storage.

- Each commercial nuclear reactor produces approximately 400-500 pounds of plutonium yearly. Dangerous for at least 500,000 years, this toxic substance poses a threat to public health which cannot be overemphasized. Present in nature in only minute amounts, plutonium is one of the deadliest substances known. In addition, it is the basic raw material needed for the fabrication of atomic bombs, and each reactor yearly produces enough to make forty such weapons. Thus, "peaceful" nuclear power production is synonymous with nuclear weapons proliferation: American sales of reactor technology abroad guarantee that by the end of the century dozens of countries will possess enough nuclear material to manufacture bombs of their own. Moreover, the "plutonium economy" urged upon us by the nuclear industry and its supporters in government presents the disturbing probability that terrorist groups will construct atomic bombs from stolen nuclear materials, or that criminals will divert such materials for radioactive blackmail. Because of this terrorist threat we may find ourselves living in a police state designed to minimize unauthorized access to such nuclear materials.

Most early developers of nuclear energy explored its potential forty years ago to produce bombs that would inflict unprecedented damage. Seven years after the United States tested two such weapons on the populations of Hiroshima and Nagasaki, the collective guilt generated by the deaths of some 200,000 Japanese civilians prompted the American government to advocate a new policy: the "peaceful use of atomic energy" to produce "safe, clean" electricity, a form of power touted as being "too cheap to meter." Together, industry and government leaders decided that nuclear power would become the energy source of the future. Today, twenty-five years later, that prospect threatens the well-being of our nation and the world.

I believe it imperative that the American public understand that nuclear power generation is neither safe, nor clean, nor cheap; that new initiatives are urgently required if we are to avoid nuclear catastrophe in a world armed to the teeth with atomic weapons; and that these initiatives must begin with awareness, concern, and action on the part of the individual citizen.

One need not be a scientist or a nuclear engineer to take part in this emerging debate; in fact, an overspecialized approach tends to confuse the issue. The basic questions involved ultimately go beyond the technical problems related to reactor safety and radioactive waste management. Even if the present state of nuclear technology were to be judged fail-safe, for example, we must ask ourselves how much faith we would be willing to invest in the infallibility of the human beings who must administer that technology. Granted, we may someday be able to isolate nuclear waste from the environment: How confident can we be in our ability to control the actions of fanatics or criminals? How can we assure the longevity of the social institutions responsible for perpetuating that isolation? And what moral right have we to burden our progeny with this poisonous legacy? Finally, we must confront the philosophical issue at the heart of the crisis: Do we, as a species, possess the wisdom that the intelligent use of nuclear energy demands? If not, are we courting disaster by continuing to exploit it?

From a purely medical point of view, there really is no controversy: The commercial and military technologies we have developed to release the energy of the nucleus impose unacceptable risks to health and life. As a physician I consider it my responsibility to preserve and further life. Thus, as a doctor, as well as a mother and world citizen, I wish to practice the ultimate form of preventive medicine by ridding the earth of these technologies which propagate suffering, disease, and death.

2

Radiation

Radiation, the particles and waves emitted by unstable elements, has saved the lives of thousands of people when used to diagnose and treat disease. But little more than thirty years after its discovery in the late 1890s, scientists began to find that radiation had a schizophrenic nature: It could kill as well as cure. Working with primitive, high-dose X-ray machines, many early roentgenologists died of radiation burns and cancer. Well known for their pioneer work with radium, both Marie Curie and her daughter, Irene, died of leukemia. Studies conducted over the past forty years have shown that many people irradiated in infancy and childhood for such minor maladies as acne, enlarged thymus, bronchitis, ringworm, tonsillitis, and adenoids have developed cancers of the thyroid, salivary glands, brain, pharynx, and larynx up to thirty years later. Studies of uranium miners and people engaged in commercial activities, as well as of Japanese survivors of atomic explosions, have yielded enough evidence to demonstrate beyond doubt that cancer of the blood, lung, thyroid, breast, stomach, lymph glands, and bone occur in human beings as a result of exposure to radiation. Today, therefore, it is an accepted medical fact that radiation causes cancer.

To understand the dangers posed by nuclear power generation, nuclear weapons production, and nuclear warfare, we must acquire a basic knowledge of the nature of radiation and its biological impact on human body cells.

All matter is composed of elements, and the smallest particle of an element is an atom. Each atom has a central nucleus consisting for the most part of protons (particles with mass and positive electric charge) and neutrons (particles with mass and neutral charge). Around the nucleus revolve electrons, particles with very little mass, and negative charge. The number of protons in the nucleus gives us the element's "atomic number"; the sum total of both the protons and neutrons in the nucleus gives us the element's "atomic weight." All the atoms of a given element have the same atomic number, but because some atoms contain more neutrons than others, not all of an element's atoms have the same atomic weight. Atoms of the same element with different atomic weights are called "isotopes." Uranium for example, with an atomic number of 92, appears in nature in two forms: uranium-235 and uranium-238.

All elements with an atomic number of 83 or more are unstable or "radioactive," which means that their atoms can spontaneously eject—or "radiate"—particles and energy waves from their nuclei. This emission process, during which an element disintegrates into other nuclear forms, is referred to as "radioactive decay," and the rate at which it proceeds is calculated in terms of "half-life." The half-life of an element is the period of time it takes for the radioactivity of any amount of that element to be reduced by half. The half-life of strontium-90, for example, is twenty-eight years. Starting with 1 pound of strontium-90, in twenty-eight years there will be ½ pound of radioactive material; in twenty-eight more years there will be ¼ pound; in twenty-eight more years there will be ⅛ pound. After approximately 560 years, the radioactivity of a given sample of strontium-90 will be reduced to one-millionth of its original potency.

In the course of this decay, atoms give off three major forms of radiation: alpha, beta, and gamma, named after the first three letters of the Greek alphabet.

The equivalent of a helium nucleus, an alpha particle consists of two protons and two neutrons. Because of its relatively great size and weight, such a particle can be stopped by a sheet of paper, tends to lose momentum quickly, and can penetrate only short distances into matter. Nevertheless, it is very energetic, and if it is moving fast enough when it comes in contact with a living body cell, it can burst through the cell wall and do serious damage to the interior. In fact, for the same amount of total energy delivered, alpha radiation has greater biological effects than any other form of radiation.

Almost two thousand times smaller than an alpha particle, a beta particle, when negatively charged, is identical to an electron. Emitted by the nucleus, beta particles can penetrate matter much further than alphas: They can travel through a number of body cells before they lose energy and come to a stop.

Gamma radiation, electromagnetic energy waves emitted by the nucleus of a radioactive substance, has the greatest penetrating power and often accompanies alpha and beta emission. X-rays are similar to gamma rays.

Radiation is insidious, because it cannot be detected by the senses. We are not biologically equipped to feel its power, or see, hear, touch, or smell it. Yet gamma radiation can penetrate our bodies if we are exposed to radioactive substances. Beta particles can pass through the skin to damage living cells, although, like alpha particles, which are unable to penetrate this barrier, their most serious and irreparable damage is done when we ingest food or water—or inhale air—contaminated with particles of radioactive matter.

Radiation harms us by ionizing—that is, altering the electrical charge of—the atoms and molecules comprising our body cells. Whether the effects of this ionization are manifested within hours or over a period of years usually depends on the amount of exposure, measured in terms of *rem* (roentgen equivalent man) units. Nevertheless, even the smallest dose (measured in millirems) can affect us, for the effects of radiation are additive. If we receive separate small amounts of radiation over time, the long-run biological effects (cancer, leukemia, genetic injury) may be similar to receiving a large dose all at once.

A very high dose of ionizing radiation (say, of 3,000 rems or more) causes acute encephalopathic syndrome —an effect scientists sought when they designed a "neutron bomb" to be used against invading forces. The explosion of such a bomb will leave buildings intact (although they may remain radioactive for years); what is destroyed is the human brain and nervous tissue. Within forty-eight hours of exposure, the brain cells will swell and enlarge, producing increased pressure inside the skull. Confusion, delirium, stupor, psychosis, ataxia (the loss of neurological control of the muscles), and fever result, combined with periods of lucidity, then sudden death.

A dose of 450 rems or more produces acute radiation illness. Thousands of Japanese A-bomb victims died from this sickness within two weeks of the bomb explosions. Such exposure to radiation kills all actively dividing cells in the body: hair falls out, skin is sloughed off in big ulcers, vomiting and diarrhea occur, and then, as the white blood cells and platelets die, victims expire of infection and/or massive hemorrhage.

Lower doses of ionizing radiation can cause leukemia five years after exposure; cancer, twelve to forty years later; and genetic diseases and abnormalities in future generations.

Of all the creatures on Earth, human beings have been found to be one of the most susceptible to the

14

carcinogenic effects of radiation.* One of America's most dreaded killer diseases, cancer is like a parasitic organism, often causing slow and painful death. It is estimated that 1 in 3 Americans now living will contract the disease at some point. During the 1970s alone, 3.5 million people were expected to die of it.

The mechanism by which radiation causes cancer is not completely understood. It is currently believed, however, that it involves damage to the genes. Our bodies are made up of billions of cells. Inside each cell is a nucleus, and inside the nucleus are long, beadlike strings known as chromosomes. Arranged on these strings are genes consisting of DNA molecules. Genes control every aspect of the individual's hereditary characteristics: hair color, eye color, personality factors, brain development, and so forth. Half of one's genes are inherited from one's mother, half from one's father.

Genes also control cellular activities, and within every cell there is thought to be a regulatory gene which controls the cell's rate of division. If our bodies are gamma-irradiated from the exterior, or if we inhale a particle of radioactive matter into our lungs and one of its atoms emits an alpha or beta particle, this radiation can collide with a regulatory gene and chemically damage it, sometimes killing the cell, sometimes leaving it alive. The surviving cell continues to function normally, until one day, five to forty years later (i.e., after the "latent period" of carcinogenesis), instead of dividing to produce two new cells, it goes berserk and manufactures billions of identically damaged cells. This type of growth, which leads to the formation of a tumor, is called cancer.

Cancer cells often break from the main mass of a tumor, enter the blood or lymph vessels, and travel to other organs. Here again, they will divide uncontrollably to form new tumors. Because they are more aggressive

---

*Because their cells are growing and rapidly dividing, fetuses, infants, and young children are the most sensitive to radiation effects.

15

than normal body cells, cancer cells utilize the body's nutrients, causing normal tissues to waste away and die.

In addition to giving rise to cancer, radiation also causes genetic mutations, sudden changes in the inheritable characteristics of an organism. In 1927 Dr. H. J. Muller was awarded the Nobel Prize for his discovery that X-radiation causes an increase in the number of such mutations in fruit flies. Muller's findings have since been confirmed by many other researchers. The genes and chromosomes of the scores of animals tested have been found to be vulnerable to radiation. The reproductive organs of human beings are believed to be equally susceptible. Moreover, the number of mutations has been shown to be in direct ratio to the total amount of radiation exposure to the gonads, whether that exposure be a single large dose or many very small ones.

A mutation occurs whenever a gene is chemically or structurally changed. Some body cells die or become cancerous when they are mutated; others survive without noticeable changes. A genetically mutated sperm or egg cell may survive free of cancer but can seriously damage the offspring to which they give rise.

There are two kinds of genes: dominant and recessive. To clarify the difference, let us consider the example of eye color. Each characteristic is determined by a pair of genes (one member of the pair coming from the mother, one from the father). The gene for brown eyes is a strong, or dominant, gene. The gene for blue eyes is weak, or recessive. A child who inherits two brown-eyed genes will be born with brown eyes. The child with one brown-eyed gene and one blue-eyed gene will still have brown eyes, because the brown-eyed gene is dominant. The only way to get blue eyes is to inherit two blue-eyed genes.

A child formed from an egg or sperm cell mutated by radiation in a dominant way will show the results of that mutation. It may spontaneously abort or, if it survives pregnancy, it may turn out to be a sickly, deformed individual with a shortened lifespan. If this person then reproduces, statistically, half of his or her children will inherit the dominant gene and its deformities. Approximately five hundred such dominant genetic diseases have been identified. A typical example is achondroplastic dwarfism: individuals suffering from this disease are born with abnormal bones, resulting in short arms and legs and a relatively large head.

A radiation-induced recessive mutation might not make itself immediately apparent. A child might seem normal but carry the deleterious gene and pass it on to the next generation. Since the disease caused by a recessive gene will not manifest unless a child inherits the gene from both parents, it might not show up for generations. Diabetes, muscular dystrophy, hemophilia, certain forms of mental retardation, and cystic fibrosis are among the 1,500 recessive genetic diseases now known.

Radiation can also cause chromosomal breakage in a sperm or egg cell, leading to seriously deformed offspring. One disease associated with chromosomal damage is mongolism, or Down's syndrome.

Deformities can also occur even when the sperm and egg cell are genetically normal, if radiation kills specific cells in the developing embryo during the first three months of intrauterine life. If a cell destined to form the septum of the heart is killed, a baby may be born with a hole in its heart. Such intrauterine damage, known as teratogenesis, can produce deformities similar to those caused by the drug Thalidomide.

We are all constantly exposed to some radiation in the form of the natural, "background" radiation to which the earth has been subject for billions of years. When the ozone layer of the atmosphere was thinner, ultraviolet rays from the sun and cosmic rays from outer space, two natural forms of radiation, streamed in unhampered to cause genetic mutations in every species. As a result, the simple single-celled organisms found in

17

the ocean evolved into more complex creatures adapted to living in the sea, on land, and in the air. Eventually the human species, with its highly specialized brain, developed. Strong or beneficial mutations prevailed, while detrimental mutations died out. Almost all geneticists currently believe that humanity has reached an evolutionary peak in the number of beneficial mutations that the species can undergo. Most genetic mutations are therefore thought to be detrimental, causing disease and deformity.

Background radiation continues to affect us. The atmosphere is now protected by a thicker ozone layer, but ultraviolet and cosmic rays still filter in (inducing, for example, skin cancer in some people when they are exposed to excessive amounts of sunlight). Background radiation also comes from other natural sources, such as the radium, radon, potassium-40, and carbon-14 present in rocks, air, and our own body cells. In Kerala, India, an abnormally high level of radioactive thorium found in the local soil is believed to be responsible for a high incidence of mongolism and mental retardation. The average level of background radiation exposure for people living in both the Northern and Southern Hemispheres amounts to approximately 100 millirems per year (6 rems in 60 years). Although the exact percentage is unknown, this radiation is thought to be responsible for a portion of all the cancers and genetic disorders afflicting us today.

Equally hazardous to our health is the human-made radiation to which most of us are exposed. Human-made radiation, too, can initiate cancer and genetic mutation. How does it reach us?

Medical X-rays are the most prevalent source of radiation for the general public today. Since the effect of each dose is additive, each exposure carries with it a minimal carcinogenic and mutagenic risk. Thus, it is imperative that doctors, dentists, chiropractors, and patients alike take into account the potentially harmful

18

effects of these rays, so that only those X-rays deemed absolutely necessary are performed. Dr. Karl Morgan, a health physicist formerly associated with the Atomic Energy Commission, estimates that 40-50 percent of all medical X-rays are unnecessary.

Nuclear power production and the process employed in the manufacture of nuclear weapons are the second most prevalent sources of public exposure. These processes result in the manufacture of hundreds of radioactive elements, which are starting to contaminate the food chain. The radioactive material finds its way into rivers, lakes, and oceans, where it is eaten by fish and incorporated into their biochemical systems, concentrating in their bodies thousands of times. Contaminated water is taken up by grass and other vegetation; again the radioactive elements are concentrated. Cows grazing on contaminated grass further concentrate the radiation and eventually pass the contamination on to us, in the form of milk or meat.

Prominent among the radioactive elements manufactured in the production of nuclear power are the beta emitters iodine-131, strontium-90, and cesium-137. Iodine-131 has a half-life of 8 days. Both this element and strontium-90 travel up the food chain, and, when ingested by humans, are absorbed through the bowel wall. Iodine-131 migrates in the blood to the thyroid gland and may cause cancer there twelve to fifty years later; strontium-90, which chemically resembles calcium, is incorporated in bone tissue, where it may lead to leukemia and osteogenic sarcoma (a malignant bone tumor). Cesium-137, with a half-life of 30 years, concentrates in animal muscle and fish; ingested by humans, it deposits in body muscle and irradiates nearby organs.

Whether natural or human-made, all radiation is dangerous. There is no "safe" amount of radioactive material or dose of radiation. Why? Because by virtue of the nature of the biological damage done by radiation, it takes only one radioactive atom, one cell, and

19

one gene to initiate the cancer or mutation cycle. Any exposure at all therefore constitutes a serious gamble with the mechanisms of life.

Today almost all geneticists agree that there is no dose of radiation so low that it produces no mutations at all. Thus, even small amounts of background radiation are believed to have genetic effects.

Similarly, there is no disagreement among scientists that large doses of ionizing radiation cause a variety of different forms of cancer. Starting fifteen years after the explosions, the incidence of cancers of the stomach, ovary, breast, bowel, lung, bone, and thyroid doubled among Japan's bomb survivors. Approximately five years after the nuclear attack on Hiroshima, an epidemic of leukemia occurred that within ten years reached a level of incidence forty times higher among the survivors than among the nonexposed population.

The direct relation between cancer and even minute amounts of radiation has best been demonstrated by the British epidemiologist Dr. Alice Stewart, who found that only one diagnostic X-ray to the pregnant abdomen increases the risk of leukemia in the offspring by 40 percent.

Every medical textbook dealing with the effects of radiation warns that there is no safe level of exposure. Nevertheless, the nuclear industry and government regulatory agencies have established what they claim to be "safe" doses for workers and the general public, drawing support from scientists who believe that there is a threshold below which low doses of ionizing radiation may in fact be harmless. This claim is dangerously misleading and, I believe, incorrect. The International Commission on Radiological Protection (ICRP) originally proposed "allowable" levels of exposure for use by the industry, but not without conceding that these may not be truly safe. Rather, it admittedly accorded priority to the expedient promotion of nuclear power. As the ISRP noted in its 1966 Recommendations (Document #2), "This limitation necessarily involves a compromise between deleterious effects and social

20

benefits . . . It is felt that this level provides reasonable latitude for the expansion of atomic energy programs in the foreseeable future. It should be emphasized that the limit may not in fact represent the proper balance between possible harm and probable benefit."

The truth is that we are courting catastrophe. The permissive radiation policy supported by the American government in effect turns us into guinea pigs in an experiment to determine how much radioactive material can be released into the environment before major epidemics of cancer, leukemia, and genetic abnormalities take their toll. The "experts" stand ready to count victims *before* they take remedial action. Meanwhile, the burden remains on the public to prove that the nuclear industry is hazardous, rather than on the industry to prove that it is truly safe.

Today's safety standards have already been shown by several studies to be dangerously high. When investigations of low-dose ionizing radiation revealed that levels of radiation lower than those permitted were causing cancer, government agencies attempted to suppress the findings.

In February 1978 an illustrative case was vindicated at a hearing before the House Subcommittee on Health and the Environment. In 1964 the United States Energy Research and Development Administration (ERDA) had funded a study to be conducted by Dr. Thomas Mancuso, a physician and professor in the Public Health Department at the University of Pittsburgh. Its purpose was to determine whether low-level radiation induced any discernable biological effects in the nuclear workers at two of the oldest and largest atomic reactors in the United States, the facilities at Hanford, Washington, and Oak Ridge, Tennessee.

Dr. Mancuso's study was one of the broadest industrial epidemiological studies ever undertaken. Over a ten-year period, he pored through 1 million files and compiled data from the death certificates of 3,710 former atomic power workers. Because of the long latency period of carcinogenesis, his first results were

21

negative; that is, he did not find an incidence of cancer higher than the norms for the general public. In 1974 the Atomic Energy Commission began pressuring him to publish his findings. The AEC wanted to use Mancuso's report to refute an independent study conducted by Dr. Samuel Milham of the Washington State Health Department; after reviewing 300,000 case histories at Hanford, he had found that there was indeed a high rate of cancer among former employees there.

Dr. Mancuso refused, claiming that his statistics were incomplete and that he needed more time. In 1975 the AEC informed him that his funding would be terminated as of July 1977 and demanded that he surrender his data to the Oak Ridge laboratories at that time. Mancuso took advantage of the interim to call in epidemiologist Stewart and her associate, Dr. George Kneale, a biostatistician, and together the three scrupulously studied the material on the Hanford workers. They came up with results similar to Milham's: a 6-7 percent increase in radiation-related cancer deaths among Hanford workers, indicating that the disease is distinctly related to radiation exposure at today's "acceptable" levels.

In fact, Dr. Mancuso discovered that the radiation "doubling dose" (that is, the dose at which the incidence of a disease is doubled) is 3.6 rads* per lifetime for bone marrow cancer, and stands at 33-38 rads per lifetime for other forms of cancer. Previous estimates, based on atomic bomb survivor data and human X-ray research, had set these doses at 100 rads for leukemia and 300-400 rads for solid cancer induction. Today every civilian nuclear worker is allowed a radiation dose of 5 rads per year: that is, workers may be exposed to doubling doses for leukemia *each year,* for cancer every *7-7.5 years.* Such figures suggest that the

---

*The *rad* (radiation absorbed dose) is a measure of radiation absorbed by a target expressed as the amount of energy (in ergs) per gram of absorbing material. The rem is a measure of the number of rads absorbed by a target multiplied by the relative biological effectiveness of the given type of radition. In this case they are almost identical.

nuclear industry will have to start hiring workers who are over sixty years of age—so that they will not live long enough to develop malignancies!

The increasing radiation exposure of workers and the general public by the nuclear industries implies tragedy for many human beings. Increasing numbers of people will have to deal with cancer or, perhaps more painful still, deformed or diseased offspring. In 1969 Dr. John Gofman and Dr. Arthur Tamplin, scientists formerly with the AEC's Lawrence Livermore Radiation Laboratory, announced that if all Americans were annually exposed to the official allowable dose of 170 millirems of radiation (the equivalent of about six chest X-rays a year) over and above background levels, there would be an increase of 32,000-300,000 deaths from cancer each year. It is difficult to predict how many mutated children will be born in the world as a result of nuclear power and weapons production, or what the nature of their defects may be. But it is indisputable that the mutation rate will rise—perhaps far higher than we would care to contemplate. The massive quantities of radiation that would be released in a war fought with nuclear weapons might, over time, cause such great changes in the human gene pool that the following generations might be severely deformed or diseased.

It is important that we keep in mind the fact that the nuclear industries are relatively young. Nuclear power has been in commercial production in the United States for only twenty-nine years; arms production for thirty-nine. Since the latency period of cancer is twelve to forty years and genetic mutations do not often manifest for generations, we have barely begun to experience the effect radiation can have upon us. Nuclear power plants and military facilities will continue to release radioactive materials into the environment, until public pressure becomes great enough to bring such releases to a halt. Because the effects of these materials on us, our children, and our planet will be irreversible, we must take action now. What we have discovered so far should serve as ample warning that our future as a species is imperiled: We are entering a danger zone—an uncharted territory—from which we may never return.

3

The Cycle of Death

Australia possesses 20 to 30 percent of the free world's known supply of uranium, the raw material upon which virtually all forms of nuclear technology depend. Following the oil embargo in 1974, the Labor Government offered to sell that uranium on the world market. Ironically, only two years earlier that same government had brought France before the International Court of Justice at the Hague and forced that nation to test its nuclear weapons underground; moreover, it had already made it the nation's policy to forego nuclear power. Now Australia publicly announced its readiness to sell the raw material for nuclear power generation for national profit.

Appalled by what I considered to be an act of misguided—and ultimately self-destructive—opportunism, I went to see Dr. Jim Cairns. Three years earlier, I had accompanied him to Paris to protest to representatives of the French government about their atmospheric nuclear tests. Now Deputy Prime Minister, he was negotiating the sale of Australian uranium with the Shah of Iran.

Dr. Cairns was a politician in whom many people placed their trust. I could not understand why he would disregard the medical dangers associated with the mining of uranium and the health hazards inherent in the nuclear fuel cycle. In discussing the matter with him, however, I realized that he was not even aware of the fact that the uranium-fission process produces plutonium, the material used to fuel atomic bombs, or that nuclear waste posed devastating health hazards.

This ignorance, unfortunately, is not unique. Over the past seven years, I have met many other politicians —in Australia, France, England, Ireland, the United States, and the Soviet Union—who were equally uninformed. Nuclear power has been with us for more than three decades. Our public servants should have taken the initiative long ago to educate themselves on this life-and-death issue. Is it not their moral responsibility to do so?

The "front end" of the fuel cycle—the mining, milling and enrichment of uranium—is dangerous, because at every step, uranium decays into radioactive byproducts which pose a threat both to workers in the nuclear industry and to the public at large.

MINING

In the United States, most uranium ore is mined in the Colorado Plateau, the Wyoming Basin, and New Mexico. During the process, two highly carcinogenic radioactive substances are released: radium and radon. Radium, an alpha emitter with a half-life of 1,600 years, is a decay product of uranium which is found in uranium ore. If radium-contaminated water or particles of the dust from uranium mines are swallowed, the radium is absorbed by the intestine and carried to the bone, where it can cause leukemia or bone cancer. Years ago, clockwork employees—predominantly women—painted the numbers of luminescent watch and clock faces using a radium-based paint. To make the figures more precise, many of them licked the tips of their paintbrushes, swallowing relatively large amounts of radium. A disproportionate percentage later died of bone cancer, leukemia, and acute radiation effects.

Radon, a gas, is a radioactive daughter isotope of thorium, which is a daughter-product of uranium. Inhaled, it can cause lung cancer. Changes in mining safety standards to protect against radon have now been implemented, but 20-60 percent of the American, German, and Canadian miners working under past conditions have already died—or will die—from cancer.

At certain levels of the Australian government, the hazards of uranium mining—and of radon—are recognized, and stringent regulations have been passed to protect miners' health. Thus, mines must be kept dust-free, and miners are required to wash their hands and faces thoroughly before they eat, in order to remove radium-contaminated dust. These hygienic measures, however, are inadequate. The miners I have spoken with said they had never been explicitly informed of the possible long-range cancer-causing and genetic effects of radiation; moreover, they reported safety regulations are not always enforced.

In 1976 I visited the only Australian uranium mine then in operation, the Mary Kathleen Mine located in hot, dry Queensland. I was given a tour and later spoke to the miners about the medical and military dangers of uranium and uranium mining. I asked the plant manager whether radon alpha emission near the men was being measured; he replied that it was not. The only radiation monitored was gamma radiation from the uranium ore at the mine face. The radon was safe, he told me, because the mine was open-cut, above-ground, and "the wind blows the dust and gas away." His rationalization was patently feeble. As we stood there, talking in the open in the heat of the day, the air was completely still; dust hung heavily around the mine and swirled about the trucks as they moved along the roads. One man was totally enveloped in dust as he sat in the open cabin of his truck while a load of freshly quarried ore was dumped into his vehicle's tray.

After I spoke to the workers at this mine, several told me that management had recorded high levels of radiation in their urine. Concerned, now that they had been informed about the dangers associated with radiation, they asked me what this condition might imply. I explained that by the time radiation is detected in the urine, it has probably already been deposited in various organs of the body—where it may have done irreparable damage.

MILLING

After uranium ore is mined, it is ground, crushed, and chemically treated. The end product is "yellowcake" (U_3O_8), a uranium compound. The waste ore, called tailings, is discarded outside the mill and left lying on the ground in huge mounds; over the last thirty years, about 100 million tons has been accumulating in the American Southwest. These tailings contain the radioactive materials thorium (half-life: 80,000 years) and radium.

Until recently, hundreds of acres of tailings thrown off from a once thriving uranium business lay on the ground in Grand Junction, Colorado. In the mid-1960s, city contractors hit upon the idea of using such tailings for cheap landfill and concrete mix. Construction firms used the waste ore to build a variety of structures, including schools, hospitals, private homes, roadways, an airport, and a shopping mall. In 1970, a local pediatrician noticed an increase of cleft palate, cleft lip, and other congenital defects among newborn babies in the area. Further investigation revealed that all these children had been born to parents living in homes built with tailings, and, when tested, many of these buildings demonstrated high radiation levels. Soon after this discovery, medical professionals at the University of Colorado's Medical Center obtained funding from the U.S. Environmental Protection Aegncy (EPA) to study the possible correlation between low-level radiation and a rise in birth defects. But a year later funds for the project were cut off: federal authorities claimed that the government had to cut back on many programs for budgetary reasons. Clearly, it did not consider the Grand Junction study worth pursuing. It is our moral responsibility to these—and all—children, however, to undertake such follow-up studies. A similar instance of laxity has occurred in Australia.

The town of Port Pirie, South Australia, once hosted a government uranium mill, which, over the years, generated some 60 acres of tailings, which were dumped in a nearby tidal dam. After the mill closed, children began using the dam as a favorite spot to practice cricket, ride bikes, and play. During the late 1960s, a company specializing in rare earth materials bought the plant, refined pure thorium from imported rare earth sands, and exported it to Japan for use in color television sets. Soon after operations began, a shipload of the material was rejected at its Japanese port of entry when it was discovered that many barrels had ruptured during the rough voyage and were leaking the thorium onto the ship's deck. Sensitive to the hazards posed by radiation, and upset by the shipper's negligence, the Japanese refused the cargo and sent it back to Port Pirie —where it was immediately dumped into the tidal dam. The dam is periodically submerged by sea water, and radiation was undoubtedly absorbed by algae, mollusks, fish, and other marine life. At low tide, children would play in the dam, crawling through the empty thorium barrels, or fish in a nearby creek.

Radiation levels were monitored at the site in 1976, when the mill was again put up for sale, and in many locations, they were found to exceed World Health Organization standards. These disturbing data were eventually leaked to the press, initiating a public outcry: parents feared their children might contract leukemia or other forms of cancer. Government officials claimed that the children were in no danger and that there was no need even to have them checked regularly for possible ill effects. The parents apparently accepted the officials' word, and no program for medical follow-up was instituted.

ENRICHMENT

Out of each ton of uranium ore extracted from the earth, 4 pounds is pure uranium. Of this amount, 99.3% is the unfissionable isotope uranium-238. Only somewhat less than half an ounce is the fissionable uranium-235. Since a specific minimal concentration of the latter isotope is needed for the fission process in most commercial reactors, but only 0.7 percent of the uranium found in its natural state is of this variety, uranium ore must be "enriched" so that its uranium-235 content comes to comprise approximately 3 percent of its bulk.

The enrichment process is extremely expensive, consumes vast amounts of energy (the Oak Ridge, Tennessee, enrichment plant consumes the electricity provided by two 1,000-megawatt nuclear reactors), and leaves radioactive tailings containing presently-unusable uranium-238. Enrichment is so costly that in the United States the federal government has to underwrite the process and operate America's three enrichment plants, located at Oak Ridge; Paducah, Kentucky; and Portsmouth, Ohio. Such subsidy has enabled this country to become the world's chief supplier of enriched uranium. It is a powerful position to hold, for it literally gives America almost complete control over—and responsibility for—the growth of nuclear power production throughout the free world at this time.

The United States may soon lose its nuclear clout, however. Not only are its uranium reserves declining, but both South Africa and France have already built small enrichment plants of their own. These foreign installations should be recognized as a legitimate cause for concern: They may well make access to nuclear fuel and the subsequent manufacture of atomic weapons uncontrollable. Approximately two tons of weapons-grade enriched uranium and plutonium have already disappeared from nuclear facilities in the United States: Some of it may have been stolen, possibly—as suggested by one CIA report—by Israel. Unfortunately, there is every indication that such acts—whether perpetrated by nations, or terrorist groups, or even criminal elements—will become a standard feature of a nuclear-powered world.

FUEL FABRICATION

After undergoing the process of enrichment, the uranium—in the form of uranium oxide (UO_2)—is converted into small pellets. These cylindrical pellets are then placed into 12-14 foot-long metal fuel rods less than 1 inch in diameter. A typical 1,000-megawatt reactor contains about 50,000 fuel rods comprising more than 100 tons of uranium in a cylindrical space about twenty feet in diameter and fourteen feet high. During the fabrication of these pellets, workers are exposed to the dangers of low-level gamma radiation emitted from the enriched fuel.

NUCLEAR REACTORS

When the fuel rods are packed into the center (or "core") of a "nuclear reactor" and covered with water, the enriched uranium is ready to undergo fission. In undergoing this process, the nucleus of a uranium-235 atom breaks apart into fragments (or fission products—the nuclei of lighter elements such as strontium or cesium), plus heat, and one or more free neutrons. The neutrons released by the splintering of each nucleus in turn break up the nuclei of other atoms. When each free neutron absorbed by a uranium nucleus is replaced by a free neutron released by another fissioning atom, the reactor "goes critical" and the chain reaction becomes self-sustaining. Control rods, which absorb the fast-moving neutrons, regulate the speed of the process.

Fission releases a tremendous amount of heat, which is used by the reactor to boil water. The boiling water produces steam, which turns a turbine—and generates electricity. Nuclear fission is thus a very sophisticated and expensive method of boiling water—analogous to cutting butter with an electric saw.

In addition to generating electricity, uranium fission throws off hundreds of radioactive isotopes—all carcinogenic and mutagenic, with half-lives ranging from several seconds to 24,400 years—or longer.

The operation of nuclear power plants presents many hazards which have been disregarded because, as frequently happens, short-term profit has outweighed the responsibility of industry and government to protect the public.

On February 2, 1976, three men with fifty-six years of combined work experience at all levels of the nuclear industry resigned from secure (and well-paying) positions as nuclear engineers at General Electric. Dale Bridenbaugh, Richard Hubbard, and Gregory Minor explained their reasons for leaving to the Joint Committee on Atomic Energy:

When we first joined the General Electric Nuclear Energy Division, we were very excited about the idea of this new technology—atomic power— and the promise of a virtually limitless source of safe, clean and economic energy for this and future generations. But now ... the promise is still unfulfilled. The nuclear industry has developed to become an industry of narrow specialists, each promoting and refining a fragment of the technology, with little comprehension of the total impact on our world system ... We [resigned] because we could no longer justify devoting our life energies to the continued development and expansion of nuclear fission power—a system we believe to be so dangerous that it now threatens the very existence of life on this planet.

We could no longer rationalize the fact that our

31

daily labor would result in a radioactive legacy for our children and grandchildren for hundreds of thousands of years. We could no longer resolve our continued participation in an industry which will depend upon the production of vast amounts of plutonium, a material known to cause cancer and produce genetic effects, and which facilitates the continued proliferation of atomic weapons throughout the world.

During their long testimony, these men claimed, among other things, that the defects and deficiencies in just the design of nuclear reactors alone created severe safety hazards, and that the combined deficiencies "in the design, construction and operation of nuclear power plants makes a nuclear power plant accident, in our opinion, a certain event. The only question is when, and where."

What makes an accident in a nuclear power station uniquely dangerous is the potential release into the environment of highly poisonous radioactive elements which can contaminate large areas of land and make them uninhabitable for thousands of years. What makes an accident seem inevitable is the human factor. The most advanced plant is still at the mercy of the fallible human beings who design, build, and operate it. Millions of parts are needed to construct a nuclear reactor, and each must be made, assembled, and operated with little room for error.

The design of a nuclear power plant is extremely complex; its construction very difficult. As the resigning engineers noted, these aspects of plant management are in the hands of specialists who do not necessarily understand the work of—or even communicate with—other specialty groups. In fact, today no one individual or group coordinates the complete process of building and operating such a reactor. The Nuclear Regulatory Commission (NRC)—formerly the Atomic Energy Commission (AEC), with no appreciable change of staff in between—is in charge of licensing and inspecting each plant. Its inspection, however, is generally confined to spot checks a few days each year. Daily responsibility for plant inspection and radiation monitoring rests with the licensees. Such an arrangement is similar to allowing restaurant owners to inspect the cleanliness of their own kitchens.

Nuclear power plants operate under many untested theoretical principles. Certain safety systems are built on the shaky test results of computer models. Many components are made of metals susceptible to failure from contact with the nuclear environment. As a result, corrosion causes cracks and subsequent leaks that are often difficult to remedy in certain sections of the plant, because localized intense radioactivity prevents entrance. The nuclear industry has avoided making certain necessary repairs by conducting computer studies which prove that a particular pipe or component part was unnecessary in the first place. In engineering language, this practice is termed a "fix."

In a nuclear plant, the repair of a mere pipe, a simple task under ordinary conditions, often requires that the plant be shut down; many workers must be called in. Some years ago, a pipe failed at the Indian Point I plant, located on the Hudson River 24 miles north of New York City. As a result, the plant was rendered inoperable for six months and 1700 certified welders—almost every certified union welder in the Consolidated Edison Company—were needed to repair the damage. It was necessary to hire that many because within a few minutes each worker would receive the dose of radiation deemed allowable for a three-to-six-month period.

Like the workers at the Mary Kathleen Uranium Mine, workers at nuclear power plants in America are told in only general terms that radiation can be dangerous; they are not informed specifically of its carcinogenic and mutagenic properties. While each person must wear a badge which monitors the level of radiation to which he or she is exposed, this device registers only gamma radiation, not the alpha or beta emissions that

33

can be swallowed or inhaled. Furthermore, workers are permitted to receive thirty to a hundred times as much radiation per year as the limit set for the general public.

At present the nuclear industry is required to keep employee medical records current for no more than five years while workers are on the job. They can be destroyed when employees leave. Radiation records must be kept, but if cancer shows up later in any of these workers, it is difficult to assess the relationship of the disease to the radiation. Medical follow-ups are rarely conducted to determine whether former employees have contracted malignancies, or to check whether their children have been genetically affected by preconception irradiation to their father's or mother's gonads. (In the event of such disability, no compensation is paid.)

At many plants the hiring of unskilled itinerant or migrant labor is a common practice. These employees work briefly for high wages, often in areas of intense radiation. After receiving their legal maximum dose at one facility (sometimes in only one day or less), they may be hired on at another plant without ever being questioned concerning their previous radiation exposure. Plants hire these transients in order to preserve the "body banks" of their full-time employees. At a reprocessing plant in West Valley, New York, which is now inoperable, "fresh bodies" were often recruited from local colleges and bars to do the industry's dirty work. From a medical standpoint, this practice is unsafe; it should be declared illegal.

The nuclear plant accident which poses the greatest threat to public safety is termed a "meltdown" or the "melt-through-to-China syndrome." Such an event could be initiated by a pipe breakage or safety failure—whether accidental or the result of sabotage—that would permit the coolant water at a reactor's core to drop below the level of the fuel rods. The rods would become so hot that they would melt; then the whole mass of molten uranium would burn through the "container" (the concrete base of the plant) and into the

34

earth, possibly triggering a steam explosion that would blow the containment vessel apart, releasing its deadly radioactive contents into the atmosphere. Soon after a meltdown with release of radioactivity, thousands would die from immediate radiation exposure; more would perish two to three weeks later of acute radiation illness. Food, water, and air would be so grossly contaminated that in five years there would be an epidemic of leukemia, followed fifteen to forty years later by an upsurge in solid cancers. The genetic deformities that might appear in future generations are hard to predict, but they surely will occur.

Such a meltdown could have staggering consequences. The Union of Concerned Scientists recently conducted a two-year study of a hypothetical "expanded nuclear economy" and concluded that before the year 2000 A.D., close to fifteen thousand people in the United States may die of minor reactor accidents. Moreover, they estimated that in the same time period there is a one percent chance that a major nuclear accident will occur, killing nearly 100,000 people; most will die of radiation-induced cancers. This study was published before the Three Mile Island accident.

The United States has already come frighteningly close to experiencing a catastrophic meltdown. In 1975, the Brown's Ferry atomic power station near Athens, Alabama, witnessed the worst accident in the history of the U.S. nuclear industry. Two electricians, using candles to check for air leaks, accidentally set fire to some highly combustible polyurethane foam used as a sealant. The fire quickly spread to the plastic coverings around the cables controlling the operation of the reactor and the emergency core cooling system, or ECCS (a device designed to prevent a meltdown by piping in more water if the coolant water in the reactor core begins to fall uncontrollably below safe levels). The blaze raged in the bowels of the plant for seven and a half hours. In the process it severed thousands of cables, knocking out most of the reactor's control systems and the ECCS. Operators watched helplessly as the water level in the

35

reactor core dropped sharply. Then, after workers resorted to equipment not intended for emergency cooling services, the water began to rise. A major disaster was thereby averted, by accident, not design.

A wide array of regulatory violations and inadequate safeguards were disclosed in the wake of this accident. First, it was revealed that the NRC had no fire hazard inspection program; only if a plant were insured for fire damage could an insurance company monitor fire-related problems. Since Brown's Ferry was not thus insured, it had never been subjected to fire-safety inspections of any kind. Second, it was eventually found that the cables were located too closely together, such that a single mishap would affect both the operational cables controlling the reactor's standard operations and the ECCS cables. Third, although the emergency menaced many lives, local citizens were never alerted— and evacuation plans were not put into effect—because no one informed the local authorities.

Another inherent deficiency that was revealed concerned the design of backup safety systems. Such systems may be redundant (that is, built of multiple but identical components) or diverse (each designed to function differently). Brown's Ferry had a redundant cabling system and five diverse emergency core cooling systems. All were disabled by the single event. At the time of the accident, Greg Minor, one of the engineers who later resigned from GE, was in charge of control design for many of the systems at Brown's Ferry. Before the fire, he considered the redundancy–diversity setup extremely reliable. The near calamity convinced him that no reactor is safe in human hands. As he and the other two engineers stressed in their testimony, "Safety features are constantly being worked on, but the tremendous cost, schedule and political pressures experienced [by the industry] make unbiased decisions, with true evaluations of the consequences, impossible to achieve. The primary focus ... has been to 'prove' the plants are safe enough for continued operations—not to openly assess their true safety."

The fact that many plants are built and operate according to the same design has been a major drawback in the development of the nuclear industry. If a safety feature in one is found to be at fault, all other plants sharing that feature should also be shut down for inspection and repair. Since the industry's inception, plants have generally spent half their time idle because of breakdowns and failures, usually involving safety-related equipment. At present the inconvenience caused by delayed service is minor, because the nuclear industry contributes only 3 percent of the United States' total energy consumption, but if nuclear power becomes the nation's major source of energy, serious problems could arise when large sections of the nation are left without electricity for months at a time. Continual brownouts and blackouts might so try the public's patience that safety concerns may be sacrificed.

The world's first nonmilitary reactor began operating in Canada in 1947 and was soon plagued with breakdowns and accidents. By the late sixties, nuclear plants in Britain, the U.S., the U.S.S.R., and Switzerland had all experienced major accidents as well, which resulted in death or injury to personnel and were potentially dangerous to the general public.

In 1957, an accident at Britain's Windscale reactor on the Irish sea released a cloud of radioactivity across neighboring fields and villages. Soon afterward, the government supervised the disposal of thousands of gallons of contaminated milk into the sea nearby. This action may have spared the public temporarily, but not for long. The polluted ocean water contaminated marine life and fish-eating mammals, and the radioactivity eventually worked its way up the food chain. Later studies revealed high levels of iodine-131 in the thyroid glands of local residents.

Following the Windscale accident, the British government compensated local farmers for the contamination and loss of their milk. If a similar major accident or meltdown occurred in the United States, however, few people would be adequately reimbursed for radiation-induced illness, or loss of life or property, because the liability of the U.S. nuclear industry is limited. In the 1950s, private insurance companies recognized that nuclear power generation was an enterprise fraught with risk: They predicted that a nuclear accident of substantial proportions could financially destroy them, and they were therefore reluctant to provide insurance. Because Congress was eager to promote nuclear power, however, it passed the *Price-Anderson Act* which absolved America's power companies of major financial responsibility in the event of a nuclear disaster. This Act recognizes that the nuclear industry could never have developed if private insurance had to cover all contingent liabilities. In fact, former Pennsylvania insurance commissioner Herbert Deneberg has calculated that if insurance companies were willing to cover the risk, the premium required to insure a nuclear plant would be about $23.5 million per year—a figure roughly equivalent to the entire current costs of plant operation and maintenance.

The *Price-Anderson Act* limits U.S. government and private corporate liability to $560 million for each nuclear generator. Claims in excess of $560 million would require legislative action. But a major nuclear accident would cause billions of dollars in property damage alone, not to speak of massive loss of life. What dollar-value can we attach to each life lost?

In the event of a nuclear mishap, individual citizens have no recourse to their own insurance firms. Most homeowner's policies include a "nuclear exclusion" clause which denies an individual compensation for a "nuclear catastrophe"—whether caused by nuclear war or nuclear power generation.

While a major nuclear accident might result from internal plant safety failures, nuclear reactors are also vulnerable to terrorist takeovers and internal sabotage by dissatisfied or simply unstable employees. A recent U.S. government study concluded—in all seriousness—that, in order to ensure adequate protection, every plant should: 1) employ a full-time guard armed with a bazooka, to shoot down any threatening helicopters and aircraft; 2) obtain the services of a psychiatrist, to assess the behavior of employees; and 3) discourage gambling among workers lest it attract loan sharks and mobsters.

In fact, when a country is dotted with nuclear power plants, enemies and terrorist organizations need no nuclear weapons to wage nuclear war; they need only drop a conventional bomb on a nuclear reactor to release all the radiation it contains, killing thousands of people. Analysts have calculated that if Europe had been powered by nuclear generators during World War II, it would still be uninhabitable due to widespread radioactive contamination of air, food, and water.

The dangers intrinsic to the nuclear industry are unique. Not only is nuclear technology unsafe, the industry has virtually ignored the fact that a reactor's highly radioactive waste products are indestructible. Were all the dangers I have enumerated thus far miraculously overcome, the sole problem of waste disposal —and its impact on future generations—should be sufficient to give pause. For, once created, some of these nuclear by-products will remain in our biosphere for thousands of years—wreaking irreversible damage on plant, animal, and human life. What moral right have we to leave such a legacy to our descendants?

4

Nuclear Sewage

The only commercial nuclear-fuel reprocessing facility ever to operate in the United States was located at West Valley, New York, about 30 miles south of

Buffalo. From 1966 (the year that it opened its doors) through 1972, the plant repeatedly violated radiation-safety standards. In October 1976, Nuclear Fuel Services, Inc., the private firm that owned and operated the facility, closed the plant permanently—bequeathing tons of radioactive waste to the citizens of New York State.

In 1977, the U.S. Congress's Committee on Government Operations spent $1 million to determine what might be done with West Valley's 600,000 gallons of high-level neutralized liquid waste and 2 million cubic feet of low-level solid waste. It concluded that the problem was "gargantuan" and might cost as much as $600–$700 million to remedy.

While in Washington, D.C., to address the 1977 Convention of the Association for the Advancement of Science, I was invited to the office of the Congressman who represented the West Valley district. To my surprise, he proceeded to ask me what I thought could be done. I replied that I did not know, for as a physician, I have no answers for the problems posed by the "back end" of the nuclear fuel cycle: the disposal of the lethal radioactive wastes produced each year by America's commercial and military nuclear programs. Nor, unfortunately, does anyone else—including the nation's nuclear engineers.

The term "nuclear waste" ("radwaste") refers to all the unusable, radioactively contaminated by-products of the nuclear fuel cycle and the weapons program. Intensely radioactive, "high-level" waste consists of fission products of uranium in the form of either intensely radioactive spent fuel or as a concentrated liquid or solid. Both forms contain substantial quantities of deadly plutonium. "Low-level" wastes include contaminated articles of clothing, decommissioned plant components, and fission by-products given off by nuclear reactors in dilute aqueous and gaseous solution; the toxicity of "low-level" wastes is said to be reduced even further by dilution into the environment.

Hundreds of radioactive elements are produced as uranium is consumed by the fission process, and these isotopes gradually build up in a reactor's fuel rods and begin to hinder its efficiency. In addition, some uranium-235 remains unfissioned; it, together with plutonium, can be retrieved and reprocessed for use at the front end of the fuel cycle. Each year, therefore, reactors are shut down so that technicians can replace one-quarter to one-third of the fuel rods.

The disposal of these "spent" rods must be carried out with extreme care, for they are intensely radioactive: a few seconds of unshielded exposure would deliver a lethal dose.

The rods are also extremely hot and must be stored temporarily in a pool of water usually located near the reactor. The water cools the rods, preventing them from spontaneously melting and releasing their poisonous contents into the atmosphere, and permits their radioactivity to decline in isolation. The swimming pool-like structures are designed to hold the spent fuel for three to six months. The rods should then be sent to a reprocessing plant in order to extract the residual uranium-235 and plutonium-239.

In 1977, President Jimmy Carter declared a moratorium on the operation of commercial reprocessing plants in the United States, in the hope that other countries would follow this nation's example and refrain from reprocessing their spent fuel to build atomic bombs. Because there are no commercial reprocessing plants in operation in the United States today, individual nuclear plants are required to store their spent fuel rods in the holding pools indefinitely, and the accumulation of such rods is causing the pools to become dangerously full. The Nuclear Regulatory Commission has granted several nuclear plants an interim license to pack their fuel rods even closer together, although a study on the safety of this procedure has yet to be completed. Such "compaction," however, may result in the production of a critical mass—causing a meltdown in the storage pool—and subsequent nuclear disaster. By the end of 1976, 3,000 metric tons of spent fuel lay in nuclear pools across the United States. By 1983, an estimated 13,000 tons will be dangerously straining the capacity of present storage pool facilities.

The U.S. military continues to reprocess the fuel in its nuclear reactors by first dissolving the spent rods in nitric acid. The solution that results is highly corrosive. Today, there are more than 74 million gallons of this high-level liquid waste in storage tanks in the United States; many of these wastes are so hot that they boil spontaneously and continuously. Most can be found at the Hanford Military Reservation in Washington and at the Savannah River facility in South Carolina. The major portion of these wastes lie in huge carbon-steel tanks which cannot withstand the waste's corrosive properties for more than twenty-five years; newer stainless steel tanks can last for fifty. But what is half a century compared to the thousands of years that this radioactive material must be kept isolated from the environment?

Moreover, many of these tanks have already sprung deadly leaks. From 1958 to 1975, twenty of Hanford's older, single-walled carbon steel tanks developed cracks through which 430,000 gallons of high-level waste leaked into the soil. In 1973 alone, an oversight on the part of a tank operator caused the escape of 115,000 gallons. These accidents may have disastrous consequences. The Hanford Reservation is located several hundred feet above the Columbia River. With no means to halt its descent, the escaped waste is migrating through the soil toward the water table and the Columbia River system, which supplies drinking water to cities in the Northwest.

Eight double-wall tanks at the Savannah River facility have shown stress corrosion cracks. In one tank, 175 cracks were detected: 100 gallons of high-level waste have leaked into the soil adjacent to the Savannah River. Local rainfall—4 inches per month—may hasten migration of the isotopes into the river.

Between 1946 and 1970, the U.S. military encased 47,500 55-gallon drums of low-level waste in concrete-lined steel drums and dumped them into the Pacific Ocean about thirty miles outside San Francisco Bay. One third of these drums are now leaking radio-activity into the Bay Area's major fishing grounds. Giant sponges, many of them over 3 feet high and believed by some to be mutants, have attached themselves to the drums.

In an attempt to minimize the corrosive properties of West Valley's high-level waste, scientists have used sodium hydroxide to neutralize the acid solution in which spent fuel rods were dissolved. Unfortunately, this procedure results in greater problems than it solves, for it doubles the waste volume and, over a period of time, precipitates a radioactive sludge consisting of strontium-90, cesium-137, other fission products, and some plutonium to the bottom of the tanks. Because of the probable high concentration of plutonium in this sludge, some experts fear that it may go "critical," initiating a reaction similar to a meltdown and releasing tons of deadly radioactive materials into the biosphere. If the 600,000 gallons of high-level waste stored at West Valley were to be dispersed in this way, the resulting radiation could devastate Buffalo and surrounding towns.

The consequences of such a disaster were foreshadowed by an accident that occurred in 1958 in Russia, at a vast nuclear complex in Kyshtym, a small town in the Ural Mountains. According to the Soviet scientist Dr. Zhores Medvedev, an "enormous explosion, like a volcano of radioactive waste" dispersed clouds of radioactivity "over hundreds of miles." He reports: "Tens of thousands of people were affected, hundreds dying, though the real figures have never been made public." The area around Kyshtym is now a wasteland, devoid of life. It will remain uninhabitable for years.

This Soviet disaster, apparently at a waste-repository site, was revealed in CIA reports which were released in 1977 under the Freedom of Information Act. It is not unfair to ask why the U.S. government covered up the occurrence of this accident for almost twenty years.

Many low-level wastes accumulate during the daily operation of nuclear reactors. Solid wastes in this category (contaminated plant equipment and clothing) are buried close to the earth's surface for easy recovery, since such burial is considered by technicians to be only temporary until safe, long-term storage facilities are arranged. Some 13 million cubic feet of solid military and research waste, containing 2,200 pounds of plutonium, are presently buried in five principal shallow-land sites in the United States, and it is estimated that by the year 2000 there will be 7 million additional cubic feet of commercial waste needing disposal. The radioactive elements emanating from these wastes are often leached into the soil by rainfall. In addition, these materials are readily susceptible to disinterment: Several years ago it was discovered that contaminated gloves, wheelbarrows, and shovels were missing from an unguarded, unmarked burial site in Nevada; it was later revealed that local citizens, totally unaware of the dangers involved, had dug up and used the equipment.

Animals that we do not use for food also act as carriers of radioactive particles. A study at the Hanford Reservation showed, for example, that jackrabbits had spread radioactivity over a wide area. They picked up the material by burrowing near trenches where radioactive waste was buried. They obviously ate or ingested some of this material, since traces of the radioactive isotopes were found in their feces. Such traces were also found in the feces of coyotes and the bones of dead hawks—animals which had apparently eaten the radioactive jackrabbits.

Government regulatory policies permit a certain amount of low-level liquid waste to be returned to the environment. Nuclear advocates and government regulatory agencies claim that this liquid effluent leaks into the environment in "safe concentrations" and that "routine emissions" of this type containing long-lived isotopes are even further diluted by the ecosphere. However, even if these isotopes are very dilute, they will inevitably become re-concentrated in the aquatic food chain.

Government agencies similarly permit a certain amount of radiation to be "routinely" emitted from a reactor stack, arguing that the gaseous radioactive effluent consists primarily of krypton and xenon, two elements that will not be incorporated into biological systems to any appreciable degree for "many years." Nevertheless, scientists are uncertain about the long-range effect of krypton emission on the environment; a gamma-emitter, krypton has been found to concentrate in the fat layers of the lower abdomen and upper thighs, near the gonads. To claim that the radioactivity in these discharges is diluted to safe levels is fallacious: it in fact adds to the existing levels of background radiation, increasing the risk of disease.

In addition to "routine emissions," "abnormal releases" of low-level radiation often occur as a result of plant accidents. Frequently reported in the press, these releases are usually accompanied by a statement from the NRC claiming that the amount of radiation that escaped was lower than the normal background radiation (the implication is that it was therefore "safe"). Missing from these accounts is the fact that any release of radiation *adds* to the level of background radiation, thereby increasing the risk of radiation-induced cancers and mutations.

Examples of "abnormal releases" abound: With a half-life of 17 million years, iodine-129 enters the food chain and eventually concentrates in the human thyroid gland. According to a report issued by the Environmental Protection Agency in 1972, the iodine-129 removal system installed at the West Valley reprocessing facility did not perform according to design. As a result, during the plant's operation (from 1966 to 1971), 45 percent of the total content of iodine-129 in the reprocessed fuel escaped into the nearby environment. At a distance of 5-6 miles from the plant, specific activity levels in animals of iodine-129 were found to be 10,000 times greater than normal background radiation; 10 miles from the plant the levels were 10 times higher. In 1976, Vermont Yankee emptied 83,000 gallons of low-level waste water into the Connecticut River. In Florida, a leaking storage pool of spent fuel rod coolant has dumped thousands of gallons into the ocean because there is nowhere the radioactive fuel could be shipped so that repairs could be made. A recent explosion at Connecticut's Millstone I plant released excessive amounts of radiation into the environment. Such accidents are reported in the press almost routinely every few weeks.

Every nuclear power plant will eventually end up on the radioactive garbage heap, because a plant can operate for only twenty to thirty years before it becomes too radioactive to repair or maintain. When the time comes for a plant's demise, it must be shut down and "decommissioned": It must either be disassembled by remote control (because it is simply too radioactive to handle manually) and its constituent parts buried, or the entire plant must be buried under tons of earth or concrete to become a radioactive mausoleum for hundreds of thousands of years. In either case the remains must be guarded virtually forever.

A nuclear reactor constructed near Los Angeles is now undergoing the delicate process of disassembly by remote control. Built in the 1950s, this small plant cost $13 million. The price of demolition is estimated at $6 million and the project will take two years to complete. Authorities have not yet determined where to bury the plant's radioactive remains.

Larger reactors (1000 megawatt or greater) may in fact be impossible to decommission. Commonwealth

Edison's Dresden plant in Morris, Illinois (at seventeen years old the oldest commercial reactor in the United States) has become too radioactive to repair. Since a new unit would cost more than $200 million, the utility is planning to clean the present plant for $35 million. The untried operation could impose serious health hazards on employees who must work in areas of high radiation.

Can we do anything to protect ourselves and future generations from the lethal legacy of nuclear sewage? At present the answer is no. Technologists have offered a number of ingenious proposals, ranging from solidification of high-level waste in glass containers and burial in salt formations, to lowering waste into ocean trenches, burying it under Antarctic ice, or launching rockets loaded with it into the sun. None of these techniques have been proven to be practical or safe.

Nuclear industry projections anticipate a total of 152 million gallons of high-level waste by the year 2000. The cost of preparing even our present load of 83 million gallons for geological disposal, however, is currently estimated at $2-$20 billion. Who will absorb these costs? At present it is not clear. The utilities want the American government (i.e., the taxpayer) to take on the wastes generated by nuclear technology. Since they do not account for the costs of decommissioning or waste disposal in their present rates, the utilities can easily present a case for "cheap" energy. Seen in its entirety, however, nuclear energy is far from cheap, and the hidden costs—to our well being—are enormous.

Succumbing to technological fervor, the U.S. government prematurely committed enormous economic resources, together with political and scientific reputations, to a half-baked technology that is neither cheap, clean, nor safe. The nation's public utilities should not have been permitted to proceed with nuclear energy production until they demonstrated that the public's health could be protected from the carcinogenic and mutagenic effects of its radioactive wastes. This was not done.

Industry engineers and physicists concede that the nuclear waste problem remains to be solved, but in their public pronouncements they urge us to trust them, to have faith in their abilities and in the inevitable advance of technology. I have no confidence in this line of reasoning. It is as if I were to reassure a patient suffering from terminal cancer by saying, "Don't worry, my medical training will enable me to discover a cure."

Nor can technology alone ever provide the answers we seek. For even if unbreakable, corrosion-resistant containers could be designed, any storage site on earth would have to be kept under constant surveillance by incorruptible guards, administered by moral politicians living in a stable, warless society, and left undisturbed by earthquakes, natural disasters, or other acts of God for no less than half a million years—a tall order which science cannot fill.

5

Plutonium

Plutonium is one of the most carcinogenic substances known. Named after Pluto, god of the underworld, it is so toxic that less than one-millionth of a gram (an invisible particle) is a carcinogenic dose. One pound, if uniformly distributed into each human respiratory tract, could hypothetically induce lung cancer in every person on earth.* Found in nature only in a remote

---

*Toxicity figures are for plutonium-239, the isotope used to fuel atomic bombs. Other isotopes are produced in nuclear reactors, including Pu-238, Pu-240, and Pu-241. The mixture is 5.4 times more toxic than Pu-239 alone.

region of Africa—and in minute amounts—plutonium is produced in a nuclear reactor from U-238 in quantities of 400-500 pounds annually! This alpha-emitter has a half-life of 24,400 years and, once created, remains poisonous for at least half a million years.

Plutonium is a chemically reactive metal which, if exposed to air, ignites spontaneously to produce respirable particles of plutonium dioxide, a compound also produced as a talcum-fine powder during fuel reprocessing. These particles can be transported by atmospheric currents and inhaled by people and animals. When lodged within the tiny airways of the lung, plutonium particles bombard surrounding tissue with alpha radiation. Smaller particles may break away from the larger aggregates of the compound to be absorbed through the lung and enter the bloodstream. Because plutonium has properties similar to those of iron, it is combined with the iron-transporting proteins in the blood and conveyed to iron storage cells in the liver and bone marrow. Here, too, it irradiates nearby cells, inducing liver and bone cancer, and leukemia.

Plutonium's ironlike properties also permit the element to cross the highly selective placental barrier and reach the developing fetus, possibly causing teratogenic damage and subsequent gross deformities in the newborn infant. Plutonium is also deposited in the testicles and ovaries, where inevitably it will cause genetic mutations which will be passed on to future generations.

In 1969 the second-largest industrial fire in United States history consumed 2 tons of plutonium at a military reactor site in Rocky Flats, Colorado. Miraculously, the fire was contained within the plant; nevertheless, plutonium oxide escaped and reached parts of Denver, 16 miles away. Radiation tests in the region demonstrated that thousands of acres of land, including a major water source, were contaminated. (Some of the soil contamination originated in 1,400 barrels of plutonium-contaminated oil stored above ground near the plant gates.) Hearings held by officials of the Colorado Department of Health in 1973 revealed that many local farm animals were being born with grotesque deformities.

The food chain concentrates plutonium many times over, most commonly in fish, birds, eggs, and milk; however, since plutonium molecules are large, they are not usually absorbed directly into the body through the gastrointestinal tract except by infants during the first four weeks of life (at which time their immature intestinal walls permit absorption). The extreme susceptibility of infants is compounded by the fact that plutonium concentrates in milk, whether from animals or humans. Chlorinated water also increases the solubility and therefore the absorption of plutonium.

Plutonium does not simply vanish at the death of a contaminated organism. If, for example, someone were to die of a lung cancer induced by plutonium and were then cremated, contaminated smoke might carry plutonium particles into someone else's lungs. When a contaminated animal dies, its polluted carcass may be eaten by other animals, or its poisoned dust may be scattered by the winds, to be inhaled by other creatures. Similarly, the same plutonium particles can go on depositing in the testicles and ovaries of successive generations of human beings, conceivably causing repeated genetic damage for up to 500,000 years, while the damaged genes are themselves passed on from generation to generation.

Plutonium-241 has another deadly characteristic: It produces americium, a byproduct with a half-life of 460 years. Americium is even more potent than its parent: Because it is more soluble than plutonium, it is more readily absorbed into the food chain. In recent years, this deadly material has been used to power more than 20 million ionizing smoke detectors, which if damaged—by fire, say—would release this carcinogenic element into the air in powdered form, to be inhaled by unsuspecting people. Manufacturers are required to demand that used and defective detectors be returned to the factory, but they do not explain the urgency of complying with this directive. What will happen to these devices? Most likely, they will end up in local dumps, where the americium will probably migrate into the soil and future food supplies.

When, in 1941, the American physicists Edwin McMillan and Glenn Seaborg first identified plutonium-239, they also discovered that it was fissionable; in other words, it was raw material for atomic bombs. Four years later the U.S. military tested plutonium's fission power on Nagasaki.

Only 10–20 pounds of plutonium are required to make an atomic bomb. Since each 1,000-megawatt reactor produces 400–500 pounds of the element per year, any nation processing a reactor could theoretically make 20 to 40 atomic bombs annually. Thus, even a small experimental facility can become an effective bomb factory. India proved this fact in 1974, when it used plutonium extracted from an experimental reactor bought from Canada to build and detonate the subcontinent's first homemade nuclear device.

Researchers at America's Oak Ridge National Laboratory have designed a simple reprocessing plant that would take four to six months to build from readily obtainable, inexpensive materials. The first 22 pounds of plutonium-239, reprocessed from spent fuel derived from nuclear power reactors, would be ready within one week. The plant would produce 220 pounds of plutonium metal per month—enough for about 20 atomic bombs.

Plutonium's role in atomic bomb production has made its value soar on the black market; it is vulnerable to theft by non-nuclear nations, terrorists, racketeers, and lunatics. Once an individual or group is in possession of plutonium, bomb fabrication is not very difficult. Using only declassified information, college students have succeeded in designing functional bombs. The designs call for metal fixtures bought at local hardware stores and 10–20 pounds of plutonium (toxic only if inhaled or ingested), an amount that can easily be concealed in a shopping bag.

Through 1980 and '81, 22 planned nuclear reactors were cancelled. Consequently, thre is now a uranium glut. But nuclear technologists look to plutonium as an eventual substitute for uranium-235 in nuclear reactor energy production. Experts had estimated that the world's supply of uranium-235 will be depleted by the year 2000. To eliminate the need for it, the industry has designed what is known as the "fast breeder reactor," which is fueled by a combination of plutonium and uranium-238. It is called a "breeder" because in the process of generating electricity, it creates more plutonium than it consumes. The average estimated doubling rate is 30–50 years; France's breeder reactor, the Super-Phoenix, is expected to take 60 years to duplicate its plutonium load.

The plutonium slated to fuel future breeders now lies in the thousands of spent fuel rods stockpiled in storage tanks throughout the world. Before plutonium can be used in a breeder, however, it must be separated from the hundreds of other waste fission products found in the spent rods. In "reprocessing," the rods are first cooled in spent-fuel pools for several months, to allow the radioactive materials with shorter half-lives to decay; the "hot" rods are then packed into strong lead containers, loaded onto trucks, and shipped over miles of highway to a reprocessing plant, where they are dissolved in vats of nitric acid. The plutonium and uranium are separated, purified, and removed, leaving behind the remaining high-level fission waste in solution. The purified plutonium and uranium are again stored in heavy protective containers, to be shipped to breeder reactor sites.

The U.S. military has used this reprocessing technique to obtain weapons-grade plutonium since the 1940s. Today, tons of extracted plutonium are routinely shipped along the nation's highways and railways, and flown into airports. In the year 2020, in an expanded U.S. plutonium economy, it is estimated that some 30,000 tons of plutonium will be produced and well over a hundred thousand rail and highway shipments will be made annually. A single accident could irradiate thousands of people.

The operation of a breeder reactor is more hazardous than that of an ordinary commercial reactor. Once out of control, a fission reaction in a breeder could cause not only a meltdown but also a full-fledged nuclear explosion. In addition, breeders are cooled with liquid sodium (rather than water), a substance that ignites spontaneously when exposed to air and is therefore highly dangerous in its own right. In 1966 a near-meltdown at the Enrico Fermi I breeder in Michigan threatened the lives of thousands of Detroit area citizens; following the incident, the reactor was shut down.

The American moratorium on the operation of commercial reprocessing plants and breeder reactors declared by President Carter in 1977 fails to recognize that such nuclear facilities are mere refinements: since anyone working in a small, properly outfitted laboratory can extract enough plutonium from spent fuel rods to build an atomic bomb, every commercial reactor breeds plutonium that could be used for nuclear weapons.

Recently President Reagan reversed Carter's moratorium. In a joint announcement made by the American Electric Power Research Institute (a research arm of the electric utility industry) and Britain's Atomic Energy Authority, scientists from both countries admitted for the first time that current nuclear reactors are producing vast quantities of waste that can be fabricated into bombs. More specifically, they acknowledged that as the radioactivity in spent fuel rods lessens over time, every spent fuel storage facility in the world becomes an increasingly accessible "plutonium mine." To deter Third World countries and terrorists from taking advantage of this situation, these scientists advocate a new method of reprocessing. Called the "civex" method, it is supposedly more effective than the previous "purex" technique because, instead of individually separating and purifying the uranium and plutonium, it combines the two elements with other fission products to create an impure mixture that is too radioactive to handle safely. Civex's advocates are convinced that this new technique will discourage proliferation, but it is doubtful. What is to stop a nation from installing a conventional reprocessing plant? What evidence is there that the threat of radiation exposure is any deterrent at all to those intent on obtaining weapons-grade material?

In 1981 the Department of Energy announced it will be extracting plutonium from commercial spent fuel for bombs because the Reagan administration plans to build 17,000 strategic nuclear weapons by 1990, and they have a plutonium storage. The ability to create plutonium by means of the nuclear fission process is one of humanity's most diabolical powers. Once created, this isotope must be isolated from the environment virtually forever. However, some plutonium—perhaps as much as 2 percent or more—cannot be accounted for and presumably escapes into the ecosphere during reprocessing, transport and other industry activities. Seaborg, the isotope's discoverer, has estimated that 1.6 million pounds of plutonium may be produced by the year 2000. Thus, by that time, as much as 32,000 pounds of the substance may be dispersing through the soil, water, and atmosphere in densely populated regions of the globe. Dr. John Gofman has shown that even with 99.99 percent storage reliability, 160 pounds of plutonium would still be released: enough cancer doses for almost fifteen times the earth's present population. If the full 2 percent were to contaminate the environment, then, in Gofman's words, "assuredly we can give up on the future of humans."

Nor is plutonium pollution just a problem of the future. It affects us all right now. In 1975 a study carried out by the National Center for Atmospheric

Research in Boulder, Colorado, revealed that more than 5 metric tons of plutonium were thinly dispersed over the earth as a result of nuclear bomb-testing, satellite reentries and burnups, effluents from nuclear reprocessing plants, accidental fires, explosions, spills, and leakages. As a result, most people in the Northern Hemisphere already carry a very small plutonium load in their reproductive organs. As plutonium contamination of populated areas worsens, that load will increase—with potentially devastating consequences for future offspring.

6

M. A. D.

(Mutually Assured Destruction)

The vision of "peaceful" nuclear power as a reliable energy source in the United States is fading fast. In 1965 the U.S. government predicted that 1,000 nuclear reactors would be operating in America by the year 2000. But new power plant orders have decreased from 20 in 1974 to none at all in 1977. Today, 65 reactors are in operation, and only 120–130 are projected by 2000.

Why is the domestic nuclear power industry not fulfilling the expectations of its proponents? The reasons are mostly economic: The price of uranium has quadrupled in the past four years, largely because multinational corporations have curtailed production to keep prices high. The cost of constructing a nuclear power plant stands at around $1.2 billion, and total plant construction time is now 10 years. Frequent shutdowns due to safety-related problems have cut the operating capacity of most plants to 45–55 percent. However, perhaps the major obstacle to expansion of nuclear energy has been the rapidly growing public opposition.

Because the dramatic decline in the U.S. market for reactors has threatened the financial survival of the nuclear industry, multinational nuclear suppliers, especially Westinghouse and General Electric, are now heavily promoting overseas trade. Their most eager customers are developing nations, such as South Korea, Mexico, Spain, Taiwan, Yugoslavia, and Brazil. Many of these countries lack the capital needed to purchase a nuclear power plant, so American loans are arranged through the Import Export Bank. They often lack power-transmitting grids to distribute the electricity generated, but the desire to produce electricity is not always their primary motivation: often their ultimate goal in purchasing a nuclear reactor is to gain access to nuclear weapons-grade materials and to join the "nuclear club." India proved this point in 1974; Israel claims to have nuclear capabilities; experts suspect that South Africa may have atomic weapons; Idi Amin claimed he would have an atomic bomb; the Shah of Iran, who commanded one of the world's largest air forces, planned to have twenty reactors in operation in 1994; and Argentina, Brazil, Pakistan, South Korea, and Taiwan have the potential to develop weapons capabilities in the very near future.

This spread of nuclear power plans around the world—and the directly related proliferation of nuclear weapons—seriously threatens global peace and order. At this writing, the United States and the Soviet Union still maintain the balance of power, but the sale of each new reactor tips the scale toward a world of uncontrollable proliferation, in which regional nuclear conflicts could draw the superpowers into all-out nuclear war.

The nuclear industry knows that the reactors it sells produce material for weapons, but its major concern seems to be corporate profit, not morality or human survival. (General Electric is known to have conducted promotional conferences with Egypt and Israel on the same day.)

Nuclear suppliers have, however, voiced concern over the use of reactor by-products for military ends: Corporate representatives from Great Britain, the United States, France, West Germany, Japan, Sweden, and other countries agreed in 1978 that any country buying a nuclear reactor and using its plutonium to manufacture bombs would receive a "reprimand." Such a scolding would not, of course, preclude further sales to the country at fault.

The U.N. is keenly aware of the weapons potential involved with nuclear power. To minimize the diversion of nuclear materials toward weapons manufacture, it passed the 1968 Non-Proliferation Treaty (NPT), whose signators agreed not to utilize nuclear materials to build bombs, or to sell such materials to any other country for that purpose. But the NPT is impotent: The world's nations are not required to ratify it, and those which have can retract their ratification with ninety days' notice—during which time a nuclear weapon could be produced.

In 1956 the U.N. established the International Atomic Energy Agency (IAEA) to police the world's nuclear facilities and deter the conversion of fissionable material into weapons. Since 1968, the purpose of the IAEA has been to enforce the NPT, but it has been given few powers to carry out its responsibilities. Agency inspectors (all too few in number) are authorized only to inspect for the misappropriation of nuclear materials for use in bombs; they are not empowered to prevent a country from actually building one. Moreover, this purportedly neutral regulatory body is *promoting* reactor sales: in 1975 it recommended that Pakistan build twenty-four nuclear plants by the end of the century.

The American government is also conscious of the "diversion" problem. The Nuclear Non-Proliferation Act, approved by the U.S. Congress in 1978, attempts to restrict foreign purchasers of American nuclear materials from diverting such materials into nuclear weapons, and calls for universal ratification of the NPT. But the new law gives the President power to override any denial by the NRC of an export license. In April 1978, for example, the NRC refused to approve the sale of enriched uranium to India because it had not signed the NPT or complied with IAEA safeguards, but President Carter promptly exercised his option and approved the deal.

U.S. government policy toward nonproliferation has been totally inconsistent. Before Jimmy Carter was elected to office, he asserted that nuclear power should be the last resort in America's quest for new sources of energy, and in his inaugural address and first State of the Union message he set the goal of "eliminating nuclear weapons from the face of the Earth." In keeping with this goal, he placed a moratorium on nuclear reprocessing and on the construction of breeder reactors. But in his proposed energy legislation, he shifted his position, calling nuclear power a safe, reliable source of energy, and allocating $1.7 billion for its development in his 1978 budget, compared to only $421 million for solar and geothermal research. The Carter Administration continues to promote and encourage nuclear reactor sales to developing countries, making reprocessing and breeder moratoriums irrelevant. Moreover, while candidate Carter attacked arms sales and opposed U.S. leaders "who try to justify their unsavory business on the cynical grounds that by rationing out the means of violence we can somehow control the world's violence," his administration has overseen a rise in U.S. arms exports of 17 percent, to a total of $13.2 billion in 1978, maintaining America's role as the world's chief arms supplier. President Reagan is actively promoting both domestic and foreign nuclear power programs.

The sale of commercial nuclear technology to the world's developing nations is an extremely dangerous aspect of the suicidal arms race that, in 1982, will move the earth $600 billion closer to Armageddon. At a rate of over $1 billion a day, nation after nation is stockpiling weapons of unprecedented destructive power, preparing the way for global catastrophe. Entrenched and self-perpetuating, the arms industry reaps enormous profits, while the world's military bureaucracies grow in political influence.

Foreign arms sales is a booming business. From 1960 through 1977, the U.S. sent arms worth $71 billion to 161 countries, accounting for almost half of all the weapons sold abroad. The U.S., Russia, France, Britain, and China continue to dominate the postwar arms race and are responsible for 80 percent of all military expenditures and foreign sales. But the sharpest proportional increase in expenditures for armaments since 1960 has occurred among the developing nations (9 percent of the world total in 1960, 18 percent in 1977)—those least able to afford such spending. Their entry into the international arms market means that military power is being dispersed more widely over the globe than in any previous time in history. The wealthy nuclear nations dominate the poor Third World, where the majority of the earth's citizens live. The result is a war system which integrates nuclear weapons with conventional arms and shifts great-power confrontations to the battlefields of the Third World.

No matter where military spending occurs, the effects are the same. Arms expenditures not only enhance the threat of global war, but divert precious resources from urgent social needs, obstruct economic growth, fuel inflation, and raise unemployment.

In today's world, 1.5 billion people lack access to professional health services. Over 1.4 billion people have no safe drinking water. More than 500 million people suffer from malnutrition. But world governments spend twice as much on armaments as on health care.

Although 700 million of their adult citizens are illiterate and 500 million (more than half) of their children do not attend school, today's developing nations are importing the most sophisticated conventional arms at a rate of $6 billion a year.

In our modern arms economy, military research consumes the creative efforts of over 500,000 scientists and engineers worldwide and gets more public funds than all social needs combined. Over half the scientists in the U.S.A. are employed by the military-industrial complex. And despite the much-publicized "energy crisis," energy research and development in the U.S. still gets less than one-sixth as much funding as weapons research.

In 1978 the developed nations spent twenty times more for their military programs than for economic assistance to the poorer countries. In two days the world spends on arms the equivalent of a year's budget for the United Nations and its specialized agencies. At present levels of military spending, the average person can expect, over his or her lifetime, to give up three to four years' income to the arms race.

In the words of Ruth Leger Sivard, former chief of the economics division of the U.S. Arms Control and Disarmament Agency, "There is in this balance of global priorities an alarming air of unreality. It suggests two worlds operating independently of each other. The military world, which seems to dominate the power structure, has first call on money and other resources, creates and gets the most advanced technology, and is seemingly out of touch with those threats to the social order that have nothing to do with weapons. The other world, the reality around us, has a vast and growing number of people living in poverty, old people who need care, more and more children who are unable to attend school, more families who never see a doctor, have an adequate dwelling, or escape from the edge of starvation. The everyday world is a global community whose members are increasingly dependent on one another for scarce resources, clean air and water, mutual survival. Its basic problems are too real, too complex, for military solutions."

While the gulf between the rich and the poor continues to widen, the poorest nations of the world, many dominated by military dictatorships, continue to arm themselves not only with weapons—but also with the capacity to produce them.

By the end of 1976 nineteen countries had nuclear reactors, including fifteen non-nuclear weapons countries. By 1984 twenty-eight non-nuclear-armed nations are expected to have reactors. Their combined potential annual production of plutonium will amount to 30,000 kilograms—enough to produce 10 atom bombs a day.

In 1946 Albert Einstein, apprehensive about humanity's misuse of the power of the atom, expressed great concern for the future of mankind. Today's nuclear arsenal must exceed his worst nightmare: Between them, the United States and the Soviet Union, alone, have deployed some 50,000 nuclear bombs which stand ready to exterminate virtually all life on earth.

When compared to the threat of nuclear war, the nuclear power controversy shrinks to paltry dimensions. A reactor meltdown might kill as many as 50,000 people; a war fought with nuclear weapons would put an end to civilization as we know it.

Conventional weapons release the molecular energies of TNT, the chemical compound trinitrotoluene. Nuclear weapons contain the explosive force of the stars: their power can be millions of times greater than conventional bombs.

Only 10–20 pounds of uranium-235 or plutonium-239 are needed to fuel an atomic bomb. Like a nuclear reactor, such a bomb operates on the fission principle: Enough of the material is brought together to form a critical mass, resulting in a chain reaction; in one-millionth of a second all the nuclei in the mass decompose, liberating the explosive power of as much as 20,000 tons of TNT. The explosion of one of these bombs over a modern city can kill 100,000 people and lay waste to an area miles in diameter.

But today's nuclear war would be conducted using hydrogen bombs. A hydrogen bomb works on the fusion principle, the same process that fuels the sun. In such a bomb, the atoms in 1,000 pounds of lithium deuteride are joined two at a time to form atoms of helium. In the process, enormous concussive force and thermal energy are released. The high temperature needed to get the process going is provided by an atom

61

bomb, which serves as a triggering mechanism, releasing more than 15 million degrees of heat. A thousand times more powerful than an atom bomb, one hydrogen bomb can kill millions of people within seconds.

By adding a 1,000-pound shell of uranium-238 to the deuterium and uranium-235 (or plutonium-239) in the average hydrogen bomb, the weapon's explosive power may be doubled or tripled at very little additional cost. The result is a fission-fusion-fission super-bomb with the explosive power of over 20 million tons of TNT. In addition to the great force and heat it gives off, such a bomb creates an enormous number of fission products which cause radiation effects long after detonation.

The explosive force in 1,000,000 tons of TNT is called a megaton. During all of World War II, a total of 3 megatons were detonated. Today, some hydrogen bombs have the explosive power of 5–25 megatons. The detonation of a single weapon of this nature over any of the world's major cities would constitute a disaster unprecedented in human history.

Today, many missiles carrying one heavy warhead have been replaced by more accurate ones carrying three to ten lighter warheads; called MIRV's (multiple independently targetable reentry vehicles), these weapons are capable of breaking away from the main rocket and landing on separate targets with deadly accuracy.

The United States has 9,200 "strategic" warheads in its arsenal today; Russia has 7,000. "Strategic" weapons are those designed by the super-powers to travel intercontinental distances for use against each other; such weapons can be launched from underground silos, or by bombers or submarines. The missiles that deliver them take off from launchpads and enter outer space; they reenter the earth's atmosphere at twenty times the speed of sound, reaching their destinations, as much as 9,000 miles away, within 30 minutes. Alerted by its military satellites, the targeted country may respond in kind by launching a counterattack. Limited nuclear war is highly unlikely. Escalating to all-out nuclear warfare using these weapons, a full-scale nuclear confrontation could last about 30 to 60 minutes from beginning to end.

"Tactical" nuclear weapons are meant for "theater" use—that is, for short-distance fighting. Russia has some 10,000 tactical nuclear weapons; the United States has 20,000, based in Europe and the countries surrounding the Soviet Union.

Tens of thousands of these nuclear bombs can be released in a matter of seconds—possibly by accident, as John F. Kennedy once warned. Over 100 near-accidents have been recorded in the past thirty years. On a number of occasions, U.S. nuclear-armed submarines on reconnaissance missions have collided with Soviet vessels; a Russian airplane carrying a nuclear weapon crashed in the Sea of Japan; a Soviet guided missile destroyer reportedly exploded and sank in the Black Sea; and an American aircraft is known to have accidentally dropped four plutonium bombs on Spain.*

Our future is vulnerable not only to human error, but also to the frailty of human emotions. A reckless national leader, or one under severe stress, could be disastrous. Several weeks before former President Richard Nixon resigned, concerned administration officials reportedly removed the mechanisms by which he could start a nuclear war. Premier Leonid Brezhnev has been treated with cortisone, a drug that occasionally induces acute psychosis.

The complex technology required by America's military and defense apparatus concentrates an enormous amount of power in the hands of a few common mortals. Spending long hours in cramped quarters, two men guard each Titan missile silo in the United States, knowing that at any moment they may receive orders to launch the missile against the enemy. Each is armed with a pistol and is under orders to shoot the other if

---

*The U.S. dug up tons of the heavily contaminated soil and buried it in trenches in Barnwell, South Carolina, where the average monthly rainfall of over 4 inches threatens to leach the buried plutonium into the Savannah River.

he exhibits abnormal behavior. Since these missiles were first deployed, thirty of these men have been seriously psychologically disturbed.

Twenty-four hours a day, in eight-hour shifts, an airplane circles near Phoenix, Arizona. It carries two senior military men holding keys that must be inserted simultaneously into a technological device to initiate nuclear war. It is hard to believe, but the future of all life on Earth could be invested in those keys.

The truth is that there are probably only two or three years before the Arms Race will be out of control. Within two years the technologists at the Pentagon will have finished developing a system called Launch-on-Warning. That means when the reconnaissance satellite detects something in Russia—maybe it's a missile going off, maybe it's an accident, maybe it's nothing—it sends a message back to a computer and then to all the missiles in America which go off within *three minutes. And there's no human input or intervention!*

Then there are the cruise missiles. They are small strategic weapons, about 10 to 20 feet long. Because they're so small they can be easily hidden and can't be counted. Up to now Russia and America could count each other's strategic weapons by satellite. That's why we got SALT II—you don't have to trust each other. Without the cruise, America and Russia—for the first time—are essentially equivalent. The cruise missile means the end of Arms Control, possibly detente, and the end of the SALT talks.

There very nearly was a nuclear war on November 9, 1979. A fellow in the Pentagon plugged a war games tape into a supposedly failsafe computer and the computer took it for real. All the American early warning systems around the world went on alert for six minutes. Three squadrons of planes took off armed with nuclear weapons. At the seventh minute the Presidential 747 command post was readied for take-off. (They couldn't find the President. He was to be notified at the seventh minute.) If in 20 minutes it hadn't been stopped, we wouldn't be here right now. And twice again, on June 3 and June 6, 1980, two computer errors nearly led us into a nuclear war. Remember, 20 minutes is currently the time limit for a retaliatory nuclear attack. This country is a sleeping giant!

What would happen if the world's nuclear arsenals were put to use?

Erupting with great suddenness, a nuclear war would probably be over within hours. Several hundred to several thousand nuclear bombs would explode over civilian and military targets in the United States (every American city with a population of 25,000 or more is targeted), and an equal or greater number of bombs would strike the principal targets in Europe, the Soviet Union, and China. Both major and minor population centers would be smashed flat. Each weapon's powerful shock wave would be accompanied by a searing fireball with a surface temperature greater than the sun's that would set firestorms raging over millions of acres. (Every 20-megaton bomb can set a firestorm raging over 3,000 acres. Theoretically a 1,000-megaton device, which has never been built, exploded in outer space could devastate an area the size of six western states.) The fires would sear the earth, consuming most plant and wild life. Some experts believe that the heat released might melt the polar ice caps, flooding much of the planet. Destruction of the earth's atmospheric ozone layer by the rapid production of nitrous oxide would result in increased exposure to cosmic and ultraviolet radiation.

People caught in shelters near the center of a blast would die immediately of concussive effects or asphysiation brought on as a result of oxygen depletion during the firestorms. Exposure to immense amounts of high-energy gamma radiation, anyone who survived near the epicenter would likely die within two weeks of acute radiation illness.

Those who survived, in shelters or in remote rural

areas, would reenter a totally devastated world, lacking the life-support systems on which the human species depends. Food, air, and water would be poisonously radioactive. Physical suffering would be compounded by psychological stress: For many, the loss of family, friends, and the accustomed environment would bring on severe shock and mental breakdown.

In the aftermath, bacteria, viruses, and disease-bearing insects—which tend to be thousands of times more radio-resistant than human beings—would mutate, adapt, and multiply in extremely virulent forms. Human beings, their immune mechanisms severely depleted by exposure to excessive radiation, would be rendered susceptible to the infectious diseases that such organisms cause: plagues of typhoid, dysentery, polio, and other disorders would wipe out large numbers of people.

The long-term fallout effects in the countries bombed would give rise to other epidemics. Within five years, leukemia would be rampant. Within 15 to 50 years, solid cancers of the lung, breast, bowel, stomach, and thyroid would strike down survivors.

Exposure of the reproductive organs to the immense quantities of radiation released in the explosions would result in reproductive sterility in many. An increased incidence of spontaneous abortions and deformed offspring, and a massive increase of both dominant and recessive mutations, would also result. Rendered intensely radioactive, the planet Earth would eventually become inhabited by bands of deformed humans scrounging for existence like troglodytes.

What would be left? Experts have projected two possible scenarios. According to one, hundreds of millions of people in the targeted countries would die, but some might survive. According to the second, the synergistic ecological effects of thermal and nuclear radiation, long-term fallout, and exposure to increased cosmic radiation would make it doubtful that anyone could live for very long. Destruction would most likely be absolute. There will be no sanctuary.

Is it not remarkable how we manage to live our lives in apparent normality, while, at every moment, human civilization and the existence of all forms of life on our planet are threatened with sudden annihilation? We seem to accept this situation calmly, as if it were to be expected. Clearly, nuclear warfare presents us with the specter of a disaster so terrible that many of us would simply prefer not to think about it. But soothing our anxiety by ignoring the constant danger of annihilation will not lessen that danger. On the contrary, such an approach improves the chances that eventually our worst fears will be realized.

The United States and the Soviet Union already have enough firepower in their arsenals to destroy every city on earth seven times over. Still, the arms race continues, the weapons multiply and become more specialized, and the likelihood of their utilization grows. Why? Because both countries, driven by fear and a mutual distrust bordering on the pathological, are locked into a suicidal strategy calling, in the words of the Pentagon, for "mutually assured destruction" (MAD) as the best deterrent to war. But "arms for peace" and "security through mass genocide" are strategies that defy logic and common sense. They epitomize our nuclear madness. First-strike winnable limited nuclear war has now become official Washington strategy.

Nuclear disarmament is the first and foremost task of our time; it must be given absolute priority. It is increasingly urgent that we find a way to achieve this goal, for time is running out. Moreover, with nuclear reactors and thousands of containers of radioactive wastes vulnerable to attack around the world, all war—conventional or nuclear—is rendered obsolete.

Our environmental circumstances changed dramatically when the appearance of nuclear weapons forever altered the nature of war. If we are to survive, we must accept personal responsibility for war and peace. We cannot afford to delegate these responsibilities to generals, politicians, and bureaucrats who persist in the politics of confrontation and in outmoded ways of thinking that have always caused—and never prevented —wars. International disputes must now be settled by reason—not with weapons.

If the 1978 United Nations special session on disarmament proved anything, it is that existing approaches to arms control are inadequate—and that it is seemingly impossible to get governments to commit themselves to genuine disarmament. It is imperative, therefore, that a mass movement of concerned citizens around the globe take up this cause and compel our governments to make nuclear disarmament the central issue of national and international politics. Joining together in an enterprise that transcends national boundaries, we in the free world must take the initiative.

Only if we abolish nuclear weapons and permanently halt the nuclear power industry can we hope to survive. To achieve these ends, it is vital that people be presented with the facts. Today more than ever, we need what Einstein referred to as a "chain reaction of awareness": "To the village square," he wrote in 1946, "we must carry the facts of atomic energy." Once presented, the facts will speak for themselves.

Out of the growing number of organizations opposed to nuclear power and nuclear arms must come a grassroots movement of unprecedented size and determination. Its momentum, alone, will determine whether we and our children—and all future generations of humankind—will survive.

7

What You Can Do

For Gunvor Refetoff (1935–1978)
who epitomized the beauty of life—
and died of bone cancer.

A human being's strongest physiological instinct is for survival. How is it, then, that the politicians, scientists, and businessmen who order, design, and manufacture the instruments of death called atomic bombs and nuclear power plants have become disengaged from their most primitive instincts? I have seen these men of might and power exhibit a sense of goodness and love at death's door: when they themselves, or a close relative, are faced with death, they become soft, gentle, frightened human beings. Many of our national leaders seem to live in a schizoid world of, on the one hand, planned death by massive genocide and, on the other, a primitive fear of death when they are personally faced with its reality. This contradiction can be explained by the powerful defense mechanism of "death denial": we all survive by pretending we will never die. Males are particularly adept at the denial of unpleasant emotions. Perhaps it is this defense mechanism that sublimates the urge to survive and allow politicians to contemplate "first-strike capabilities" or "limited nuclear war"—in which the deaths of twenty million Americans or Russians are deemed "acceptable."

My experience with national political leaders has not inspired me with confidence. I find that they are generally ignorant of the major medical and scientific ramifications of their decisions. They are manipulated by powerful, well-financed industrial and military lobbies. Driven by power and the need for ego-gratification, they are, to a large degree, desensitized to reality. This vision is limited to their meager two-to-four-year terms of office; the desire for reelection influences all their decisions. I have found, sadly, that a global view of reality and a sense of moral responsibility for humanity's future are very rare among political figures.

Even after Watergate, Vietnam, and CIA exposés, the American people still seem to trust their political leaders. When I speak at church meetings, describing the enormity of our nuclear madness, people approach me and ask, "The politicians don't know this, do they? Because they wouldn't let any of this happen if they did." I look them in the eye and tell them that their government is totally responsible for organizing this calamity.

But if we can't trust our representatives, whom can we trust? The answer is simple: No one but ourselves. We must educate ourselves about the medical, scientific and military realities, and then move powerfully as individuals accepting full responsibility for preserving our planet for our descendants. Using all our initiative and creativity, we must struggle to convert our democratic system into a society working for life rather than death.

"But," people often say, "it is impossible to change the system." I do not agree. I informed the Australian public about the medical dangers of fallout, and the federal government was finally forced to take France to the International Court of Justice. Three years later I pressured the government by teaching the nation's workers about the medical and military hazards associated with uranium mining. By September 1977 the Australian Council of Trade Unions (the executive body of the Australian Union movement) had passed a resolution declaring that unless the federal government agreed to fund a year-long nationwide debate and subsequent referendum on the wisdom and safety of uranium mining, no Australian worker would mine, transport, or load the stuff onto ships for export. The

70

Australian Waterside Workers Federation voted unanimously to support the boycott; the Australian Railways Union refused to touch the material. In December 1977 the Australian Labor Party (which by then opposed the mining and selling of uranium on the open market, although two years earlier it had been in favor) announced that, if returned to office, it would ban the mining and treatment of uranium in Australia until adequate nuclear-waste safeguards were developed and until a satisfactory national debate had taken place. Nor would it allow the opening of any new mines. Moreover it promised, if elected, to cancel all the uranium contracts that the present Liberal Party government has signed with other countries.*

Few Americans are aware that in June 1977, 80,000 people marched in the streets of Australia's capitals, demanding that uranium be left in the ground: In Australia, despite the fact that huge profits would be reaped by overseas uranium sales, democracy has been mobilized to fight for human survival. From October to December 1981 in Europe, over 2 million people marched for nuclear disarmament.

Nuclear power and nuclear war are primarily medical issues. Arguments about profits, jobs, and politics are reduced to irrelevancy when our children are threatened with epidemics of leukemia, cancer, and inherited disease—or sudden death, in the case of nuclear war. What will be the cost of hospitalizing all the people who contract these terminal diseases? The medical expenses incurred will far outweigh any enonomic benefits gained by this generation—to the detriment of all those that will come in the future. But of course no human

*Many of Australia's richest uranium deposits are found on sacred aboriginal tribal lands. Government efforts to further expropriate such lands continue a heartless process of cultural and religious persecution against these shy and innocent people, for whom the Australian continent has been home for millennia. Aboriginal "dream-time" myths describe a "rainbow snake" said to live on uranium-rich Mount Brockman. If disturbed, the snake would bring great disaster both to the local aboriginal and white populations, and also, it is believed, to the world at large.

life can be measured in dollars. Who would care to put a price on his or her own life? Each life is precious, unique, and invaluable—a truth brought home to me each time I see a baby born or a child suffer and die from leukemia or cystic fibrosis.

I am often asked what the medical profession is doing about the public health hazards posed by nuclear power and weapons production. I firmly believe that it should take a strong and unequivocal stand in opposition to the technologies of death. Unfortunately, my experience in the atmopheric-test campaign in Australia taught me that although most doctors readily conceded that radiation poses a growing public health hazard, few were willing to support the public stance that I had taken (most dismissed it as naive and doomed to failure) and fewer still were willing to give political meaning to their Hippocratic oath by speaking out themselves. I have found a similar reluctance among physicians in the United States, based in large part on a lack of information about the nuclear fuel cycle and the extent to which public health is threatened by the spread of nuclear power plants. Medical schools and journals do the general public a disservice by neglecting this major health issue.

When I have addressed the issue of nuclear power at medical meetings in America, however, the response has always been generally supportive. In 1975, for example, the New Hampshire Medical Association invited me to speak about the medical dangers of nuclear power at one of their monthly meetings. The doctors present understood the medical dangers of radiation, but they did not know the intricacies of the fuel cycle and the special radioactive health implications involved at each stage. They were generally unaware of the massive quantities of different radioactive isotopes produced as nuclear waste, and they really did not know that the storage of nuclear waste remains a serious, unsolved dilemma. After the lecture and subsequent discussion, these doctors were convinced of the gravity of the situation, and several who had posed the most searching and difficult questions approached me. As they shook my hand, I noticed that they had tears in their eyes. They thanked me and wished me luck. Several weeks later, six wrote a letter to a major New Hampshire newspaper stressing the long-term medical dangers of nuclear power—provoking a stormy response from the nuclear industry. Because of the public controversy, many people became aware that nuclear power is *not* safe: after all, even their doctors saw it as a health hazard. We need more such controversies, engendered by doctors, nurses, and other health professionals dedicated to the practice of preventive medicine and the eradication of radiation's biological hazards from the environment.

It is currently believed that 80 percent of all cancers are caused by environmental factors. By definition, therefore, they are preventable. The U.S. government spends millions of dollars each year funding medical research into the cause and cure of this dreaded disease. At the same time, however, it spends billions funding the weapons and nuclear power industries—which propagate the diseases doctors are struggling to conquer. We in the medical profession must begin to practice what I call "political medicine," something we are not trained to do. Political medicine opposes industrial practices which contaminate the environment with disease-causing agents. In this way it attempts to attack the "front end" of the cancer cycle and prevent the disorder from occurring—rather than trying to cure malignancies after they are diagnosed, when it is often too late.

In the past three years, 10,000 physicians have joined Physicians for Social Responsibility to educate colleagues and the public about the medical consequences of nuclear war. The American Medical Association in December 1981 passed a resolution condemning nuclear war and pledging to educate the President and members of the congress and senate on this subject.

America's scientific community has a unique obligation to assess the morality of its work and to assist the public to understand the perils we face: in the event of nuclear holocaust, it is science that will have led us down the road to self-destruction. The first meltdown or nuclear-waste explosion will disprove, once and for all, the blithe assurances offered by industry experts regarding reactor safety and waste-disposal technology, but only after bringing tragedy into the lives of thousands of human beings.

The Industrial Age has enthroned science as its new religion; the scientific establishment has, in turn, promised to curse disease, prolong life, and master the environment. Thus, humanity now believes that it owns the earth; we have forgotten that we belong to it, and that if we do not obey the natural laws of life and survival, we will all cease to exist.

Unfortunately, my experience has taught me that we cannot rely upon our scientists to save us. For one thing, they do not preoccupy themselves with questions of morality. For another, science has become so specialized that even the best scientists are immersed in very narrow areas of research: most lack the time to view the broad results of their endeavor, let alone the willingness to accept responsibility for the awesome destructive capabilities science has developed. When confronted with the realities of our nuclear insanity, they are often either embarrassed or display a cynical fatalism, saying that humanity was not meant to survive anyway. Since about half of America's research scientists and engineers are employed by the military and related industries, they suffer from a profound conflict of interest: many simply prefer not to ponder the consequences of their work too deeply; after all, they have to feed and educate their children—a strange reaction, considering that, as a direct result of their research, their children may not live out their normal life span.

Many scientists *have* stood up to the nuclear establishment, but only at great cost to themselves and their families. Journalist Jack Anderson has observed that these "courageous scientists—Thomas Mancuso, John Gofman, Alice Stewart, George Kneale, Samuel Milham, Arthur Tamplin, Ernest Sternglass, and Irwin Bross—have come under malicious attack reminiscent of the campaign against Hollywood and Broadway liberals during the anti-communist hysteria. We have tried to tell the story of these scientists whose cautious warnings have been assaulted and belittled, whose personal reputations have been besmirched." Why has this happened? Because, he notes, "The stakes are enormously high. Both the federal government and the nuclear industry are committed to developing nuclear power. Too many unfavorable stories would jeopardize the industry's multibillion-dollar investment ... Government officials have also staked their careers on the development of nuclear power. They would look foolish if their massive efforts had to be scrapped because they underestimated the dangers of low-level radiation. Not only would the billions spent on nuclear projects have to be written off, but additional billions might have to be paid in compensation to those whose health has been impaired." This intimidation ritual would be less popular with government if more scientists were to accept their moral responsibility to teach the public about the technological dangers to which science has exposed the world.

I spent one of the most important and inspiring evenings of my life in January 1976, talking with three men and their wives. The men were about to sacrifice their life's work and secure employment for the sake of a principle that involved the future of the human race. They were Dale Bridenbaugh, Gregg Minor, and Dick Hubbard, the three nuclear engineers about to resign from General Electric. As we sat together, discussing the ramifications of their decision upon their families, their lives, the nuclear industry, and the world at large, I could see the pain of uncertainty on their faces as they contemplated the future. Over the years, they had gradually realized that their highly paid and socially respectable jobs were an integral part of an entrenched multibillion-dollar industry which threatened future generations. Their wives were also worried about the impending resignations, and the possibility that their husbands would have difficulty finding stable employment. They realized that they would have to reduce their accustomed standard of living. But each of these women was totally committed to the decision; in fact, it was they who had first posed the unanswerable moral questions relating to the spread of nuclear power. These men and women demonstrated courage and self-sacrifice in the name of human survival. They stand as models that more members of the world's scientific and engineering communities should emulate.

How is it that the brilliant efforts of American scientists have been put to destructive uses? How did American culture become so embroiled in the death cycle? When Pearl Harbor was bombed, the Japanese declaration of war was delivered to the American Secretary of State half an hour after hostilities began. The Japanese admiral Yamamoto was devastated by this diplomatic breach of protocol, and said, "I fear we have awakened a sleeping giant and filled him with a great resolve." I think the American people were so shocked by the unprecedented devastation of Pearl Harbor that they resolved never to be vulnerable again. That is why America's politicians developed a nuclear arsenal after 1945, even though nuclear scientists pleaded that it not be developed. But the drive for invulnerability leads to total vulnerability. A valid concept of national security should ensure life and a healthy future for the human race. Instead, the Pentagon scenario of national security through mutually assured destruction assures our annihilation.

I am very worried by the fact that most Americans are not aware of the realities of their present-day existence. As I speak to thousands of citizens, I find that they generally know next to nothing about the medical effects of nuclear power and have entirely suppressed the atomic bomb anxiety that pervades the rest of the world. The Kennedy-Khrushchev talks began to thaw the Cold War, but when Kennedy was killed, the world was devastated—not just because a popular president was slain, but because he had initiated a new era which sought to move away from nuclear brinksmanship. The international grief was compounded by fear for the future. As Lyndon Johnson took over the reins of government and enacted the Civil Rights program, however, somehow world attention was diverted from atomic bombs. Vietnam reared its ugly head, and Watergate became the overriding issue of the early '70s. During those years, it was a relief to think about "manageable" problems and forget the unthinkable. People became ostrichlike and pretended the nuclear threat had ceased to exist. Meanwhile, the Pentagon, always five years ahead (with Russia striving to keep up), quietly continued refining and building more and more atomic and hydrogen bombs, delivery systems, satellites, submarines, et cetera. In reality, nuclear madness had not disappeared: it multiplied.

Still, most Americans remain strangely silent, as if mesmerized into a feeling of safety and security. I find this self-delusion difficult to understand. On the one hand, I know several people, including two physicians, who have recently lived in Russia for a number of years. They report that almost every Russian with whom they made contact spoke spontaneously of a fear of the imminence of atomic war. Unlike Russia, which was invaded and lost twenty million people in World War II, this country has never suffered the total devastation of a massive military conflict, and I think this is the reason why the immediacy and danger of war is alien to American psychology. This society is geared to the joys of short-term satisfaction, with "happiness" projected as the ultimate goal of human existence. Death is denied by painting corpses to look like living flesh, by using expressions such as "passing away," or by arranging for people to die in impersonal hospitals away from the family. The tearing pain of grief is avoided at whatever cost. But death is a reality that must be faced, and war is an ever-present danger that must be confronted if we are to avoid it.

But what about the Russians? Every time the Pentagon needs more money, the Russian spectre is called up. The reality is that if both superpowers, together with the lesser powers, continue on this mad spiraling arms race, building more and more atomic bombs, sooner or later they will be used. We cannot trust in the sanity and stability of world leaders. (In fact, great power tends to attract disturbed individuals.) Recent history abounds with examples: Hitler, Mussolini, Stalin. Meanwhile, we are racing like lemmings toward mutually assured destruction. Someone must make the first move away from death and toward life. Do we really have anything to lose? We are doomed if we don't—but we may save the human race if we do. The elimination of nuclear weapons should be a national goal. I believe that the Russian people are so frightened of nuclear war that they would heave a momentous sigh of relief and would want their own leaders to follow America's moral initiative toward nuclear disarmament.

What is happening to our society? Even America's schools are being used by the nuclear industry for massive advertising campaigns: each year every high school in the U.S.A. is visited by a utilities expert, who subtly indoctrinates his listeners in the belief that nuclear power is "safe." It is my understanding that such advertising in institutions of learning is illegal; if it is not illegal in the United States, it should be. I have watched utilities representatives put on one-man-shows before auditoriums filled with high-school students. As props they use a simulated nuclear reactor and various other machines which use electrostatic energy to make the children's hair stand on end. They tell their audience that nuclear power is safe, clean, and efficient—and that plutonium is safe enough to hold in the palm of one's hand. On several occasions I have addressed students after an industry representative spoke; I described the real dangers posed by nuclear power. The children were obviously fascinated by the machines and the technology pertaining to the industry, but they became quietly sober after I had spoken. One representative told me, "I don't usually discuss morals when I talk to children about nuclear power. I'm not used to this." It is a disgrace that the nuclear industry should be allowed unlimited access to the gullible young, when it amounts to teaching children to accept and support nuclear power.

I spoke at many schools in Australia about uranium, and the young people there were very enthusiastic and receptive. Many joined anti-uranium groups and were particularly good at knocking on doors and talking to their neighbors.

My experience in this country has already taught me that established government institutions are hard to budge. In 1975 I wrote to each member of the U.S. Congress Joint Committee on Atomic Energy to ask if I could talk to the committee about the medical implications of nuclear power. My offer was never formally acknowledged, but I received some interesting replies from individual members, justifying nuclear power because the nuclear submarine program had been so "successful." I was told subsequently by an administrative assistant that the committee had never heard testimony from an independent medical doctor about the medical implications of nuclear power, but only from members of the staff of the NRC and ERDA, so they were relatively ignorant of the basic radiobiological implications of nuclear energy. I might add that the Watergate investigation revealed that Gulf, Ashland Oil, and the Northrop Corporation, subsidiaries of which are leading suppliers of nuclear technology, were found guilty of making illegal "political contributions" to politicians in America and abroad, dispersing well over $10 million. The recipients of these illegal funds included key representatives and senators who were serving at the time on the committee. Clearly, illegal payments of this type make many state and federal legislators less than objective when voting on nuclear issues. Such bribery may partially explain how nuclear technology—although unsafe and uneconomic—could have been supported by so much favorable legislation over the years.

When contacted, the White House public liaison office assured me that this was an open administration —if you approached it the right way—and advised me to send a memo to Jimmy Carter. I sent a single-page document, briefly outlining the genetic, carcinogenic, teratogenic, and military properties of plutonium, and ended by saying, "I strongly urge your further investigation of this subject and I would like an opportunity to convince you of my concern." It was three weeks before I received a letter from the public liaison officer, giving me the name of a doctor employed by the Energy Research and Development Agency (ERDA) who, I was told, would be pleased to speak to me if I so desired. I didn't bother to make an appointment: ERDA is totally devoted to the expansion and development of nuclear power (it oversees the manufacture of atomic weapons, including the neutron bomb), and any doctor who works for that agency has already sold his soul to the devil.

The high-level bureaucrats serving in ERDA and on the Nuclear Regulatory Agency (NRC) are—and have always been—notoriously pronuclear. A 1976 Common Cause study revealed why industry preferences have received so much favorable treatment: Half of ERDA's top employees have been recruited from corporations with interests in energy development, and all nine executive positions have been filled by former employees of ERDA and NRC contractors; the NRC, meanwhile, has drawn more than half of its employees from corporations, laboratories, or universities under its supervision—including the U.S.'s "Big Five" reactor suppliers (Babcok and Wilcox, Combustion Engineering, General Atomic, General Electric, and Westinghouse) and other multinational corporations (such as

Rockwell International, DuPont, Bechtel, Allis-Chalmers, and General Dynamics) which profit from nuclear expansion and generous regulatory decisions. How can truly objective decisions regarding nuclear technology be made by agencies so rife with conflict of interest? They cannot.

The huge multinational corporations comprising the atomic industrial complex influence our elected representatives and appointed officials, through massive federal and state lobbying efforts which reflect their immense power and wealth. Financed by earnings reaped from a variety of technologies that are harmful to the environment and public health, such lobbying can subvert the democratic process by compromising the public interest in favor of the accumulation of ever more profit. As long as our democratic system prevails, however, the general public has an effective recourse in the form of the electoral ballot. The burden lies upon the electorate to become better informed about its genuine long-term interests, and then to make its demands known. Public education is the first step, to be followed in part by a grass-roots lobbying effort (in the form of a letter-writing campaign) and personal meetings with elected officials.

In 1976 I wrote to every federal and state politician in Australia, warning of the dangers of uranium mining. I enclosed a brief summary of the medical, military, and genetic implications of uranium mining and closed with a statement that this was the most important issue ever to face the human race, and that "they and their colleagues would go down in history either as great statesmen, or alternatively, as those politicians who made a disastrous mistake." Although most of the replies reflected party lines (to export or not to export), at least all these people were made more conscious of the medical hazards presented by uranium. Some asked for more detailed information; others contested that nuclear power is as safe but more practical than solar energy. Almost no one addressed the proliferation of nuclear weapons. Several months later I sent all these federal politicians a copy of "The Plutonium Economy," a critical report prepared under the auspices of the American National Council of Churches, by a committee co-chaired by Margaret Mead and including several Nobel laureates. As a concerned citizen I felt it my duty to educate my political representatives.

We need to educate the politicians in America, by making sure they read about the biological effects of nuclear fission products and nuclear waste and the medical consequences of nuclear war—and I mean *every* federal and state politician in the United States. It is imperative that our political representatives be educated regarding the long-term consequences of their nuclear-related decisions. Because such decisions exert their effects for millennia, they must not be influenced by considerations of short-term self-interest. The public must enable its leaders to understand and reflect popular opinion.

It is of vital importance to educate the workers of this country, as well, because they are the grass-roots members of our democracy and the true power behind this system. Because only 20 percent to 30 percent of America's workforce is unionized, reaching America's nonunionized workers, in particular, will require a massive effort, but that effort must be made. Contacts can be forged with factory operators and managers. Workers should be taught by knowledgeable, caring people. I urge America's labor unions to utilize their education committees to inform their members of the lethal hazards posed by nuclear power stations and weapons production. The irresponsibility of the nuclear industry to its own workers should be emphasized: Every potential employee of a nuclear facility, whether civilian or military, should be fully informed about the dangers to which he or she will be regularly exposed, and of the necessary precautions that must be taken in the workplace.

The argument is always raised that we need to build nuclear power plants and bombs to provide people with jobs. The truth is that the nuclear power and weapons industries are capital-intensive, labor-disintensive: that is, they provide relatively few jobs per dollar invested. The money needed to enrich uranium, build nuclear plants ($3 billion is needed for California's new Sun Desert facility), decommision reactors, and store wastes for half a million years would employ many more people in industries building solar panels, growing food, feeding the world's starving children, building mass transit systems, and rebuilding cities. The same is true for the weapons industry. The logic of the argument that it is important to build death industries to supply jobs which will eventually kill the people who hold those jobs—and their children—escapes me.

My success with the Australian labor movement prompted me, upon my arrival to the United States, to write George Meany. Expecting the attitudes of America's unions to be similar to those of Australia, I had hoped to forge a link with America's labor movement through Mr. Meany's good offices. To my distress, I received a reply from one of Mr. Meany's special assistants informing me in no uncertain terms that, because of the severity of America's energy crisis, the AFL-CIO supported the expansion of the nuclear power program and did not subscribe to the idea that radiation causes cancer. Further correspondence and other contacts underscored the degree to which the AFL-CIO is tied to industry-government policy.

Mr. Meany's argument is mistaken: The single most effective way of overcoming the world's energy crisis is through oil conservation in the United States, coupled with the development of alternative energies. At present, the American people, comprising only 6 percent of the earth's population, consume one-third of all the oil used in the world every day, *and consumption has been rising!* Daniel Yergin, a member of the Energy Research Project at the Harvard Business School, points out that "The amount of energy used per person in Sweden is 60 percent of the amount used per person in the U.S. In West Germany, the figure is 50 percent, in France less than 40 percent. This does not mean that we could instantly achieve the efficiency of those other countries in energy use. But these comparisons ... suggest that we could use a good deal less energy— 30 percent to 40 percent—*without cutting into our standard of living*. Such changes," he continues, "would call for new investment ... But they would involve a good deal less investment and much shorter lead times than do oil or nuclear reactors."

My experience with Australia's unions confirms my belief that, when presented with the facts, workers will opt for health and safety. Seventy-five percent of Australia's workers are unionized, and at the outset of the anti-uranium mining campaign I wrote to each of South Australia's seventy-six unions (including the boiler makers, plumbers, pastry cooks, railway and metal workers) requesting an opportunity to address their memberships. Warning me that the need for jobs made it highly unlikely that I could convince them that uranium mining should be banned, they nevertheless agreed to hear me out. By September 1976 the Australian Council of Trade Unions had passed its fateful resolution.

Because of the contact I had made with the unionists in Darwin, I arranged a visit with the Trades and Labor Council there in order to have more immediate contact with the workers who would be most directly involved in opening and working the new Ranger mines in the Northern Territory. The Council was very receptive and has since become committed to a no-mining policy. The workers responded extremely well to my simple lecture on genetics and radiobiology.

On the same trip, I arranged with the Queensland Amalgamated Metal Workers Union to visit Mary Kathleen, a village in central Queensland that is the site of Australia's only working uranium mine. I was apprehensive as I flew across the dry, barren outback in a small, single-engine plane, because the miners at Mary Kathleen lived in a nice little town that enjoyed all the modern conveniences. They were deeply committed to mining uranium and had threatened to tar-and-feather the next person who tried to convince them that mining the ore was dangerous. Tempers were hot among the supporters of uranium mining in Australia, and I knew these people meant what they said. But I also know that they had to be spoken to by a physician, if they were to comprehend the full significance of uranium for themselves, their families, and future generations.

I was driven to the mine by several members of the Australian Amalgamated Metal Workers Union—strong, mature men in whose company I felt relatively safe. My first stop was company headquarters, where I spoke to the mine's manager. He was courteous but cold. Eventually he relaxed, and after answering some questions related to radiation-monitoring and workers' safety, he took me up to the mine face. Later we went down to the village of Mary Kathleen, where I was to speak to the workers. We stood in the town square, listening to numerous transistor radios forecasting the results of the Ranger Government Inquiry on Uranium Mining, a report that had been prepared by a three-man commission appointed to collect evidence from hundreds of Australians on the benefits and dangers of mining uranium ore. Both the federal government and the general public awaited the report with eager anticipation. Most of us felt that it would rule against uranium mining. The Mary Kathleen miners were apprehensive as the broadcast began, but when it was announced that the Ranger Inquiry had given a green light to uranium mining, miners jubilantly cheered. I felt nauseated, and a sense of impotence and despair descended upon me. Nevertheless, I summoned my energies to address the workers and their families about the medical dangers they faced.

Although many people were celebrating with mugs of beer and a lot of noise, they quieted down as I began speaking. Once again I talked about radon gas and lung cancer, radium and leukemia, stressing the fact that they had to be extremely careful to wash their hands and faces before eating. I went on to explain each step of the nuclear fuel cycle, and the serious dangers posed by nuclear waste (and nuclear war) to unborn children. They listened in silence, applauded at the end, then lined up to ask me questions. Several men told me that radiation had been detected in their regular urine tests, and wanted to know what that might mean. One of these men was only twenty-six years old and had a strong family history of cancer. I told him that if radiation was detected in his urine, it was probable that some radioactivity was already present in his body, and because of his probable inherited predisposition to cancer, he should leave the mine immediately. The men in general seemed very concerned; only one remained hostile to the end. They offered me a drink, and I think I would have been there all night, answering questions, if my union friends had not dragged me away.

I felt the trip had been successful. I had not been tarred and feathered. The reception had been polite, and the men learned of the many dangerous facets of their work, about which they had been totally ignorant. Subsequently the miners demanded that a health clinic be established at Mary Kathleen. Several resigned, and later a strike was held to demand improved conditions.

The Australian unions are among the most receptive and responsive people that I have talked to so far.

Nuclear workers throughout America are starting to worry about the effects of radiation exposure. Reports of higher-than-normal cancer rates at the Hanford, Washington nuclear installation led workers at Buchanan, New York's Indian Point Consolidated Edison station to begin expressing these fears. "I accepted a temporary assignment three years ago without knowing what it could possibly do to me," said one welder. "I hear top scientists saying now that there are no safe levels of radiation and I don't want to wind up as somebody's mistake." I find that the work force here tends to accept such dangers in a remarkably trusting manner. It has been reported that nuclear submarine workers at Portsmouth, New Hampshire, are developing cancer at a very high rate, double that for representative men of the same age. I was invited to speak to a meeting of these workers, but only four men appeared. They told me that the navy had threatened them with the loss of their jobs if they came to hear me speak. I felt sorry for the men who didn't come, who feared more for their jobs than for their lives.

Media, the most effective way to reach the members of a democracy and the most powerful influence in America today, expose the masses to bland trivia and brainwashing. The subliminal effects of media propaganda and advertising teach people to desire what they don't need and to strive for materialistic pleasures. Communication and family relationships suffer as a result; people tend to be relatively shallow and spoiled, always desiring more of everything, but somehow unable or reluctant to comprehend the moral degradation of a world in which millions can be killed by the press of a button, a world in which two out of every three children are malnourished and starving. A longterm sense of responsibility toward the continuity of life is not evident in America. Life has become so easy, with everything ready-made or instantly served, that the true soul and center of the individual seems to have atrophied. People lack the resilience to face reality.

Television is the most important shaper of opinion in American society today. It is presently used to promote the activities and profits of the multinationals. It is supported and controlled by big business, and the vision of the American way of life it portrays has been carefully molded to comply with the profit motives of America's corporate leaders. Programming is developed to support and carry advertising; its standards often promote the low, banal, trivial, violent, and pornographic. The intellect, curiosity, responsibility, and self-reliance of the American people are rarely stimulated or acknowledged on most TV programs. How, therefore, can a mesmerized public be stimulated to learn about the true state of the world, and to become aroused and motivated to use democracy constructively, for survival?

In Australia, we were very successful in utilizing the media to inform the public—at no cost. All the exposure we received was free. Radio call-in shows, for instance, are ideal for voicing opinions and bringing provocative issues to public attention. They can also be used to advertise marches. We usually organized big ones once every six weeks, always obtaining a permit from the police department. We demonstrated on Saturday morning, during peak traffic time, when everyone went shopping. On Fridays we would use the call-in shows to advertise the march. We were often interviewed by local, popular commentators about some aspect of the uranium question, and at the end of the interview we would always tell the listeners that if they wanted to do something about this terrible problem they could join the march to be held the next day—always making sure to give its time and place.

At the conclusion of each march, we would have several prominent people give short, fiery speeches, and then announce the date of the next demonstration. Over a period of nine months, the number of participants at these marches grew from several hundred into the thousands. Banners above the crowd proclaimed "Geologists Against Uranium"—or "Teachers," "Railway Unions," "Housewives," "Clergy." Other signs read "Nuclear Power Equals Cancer."

The television and radio stations started covering our marches regularly, because they were becoming important political events. People would often be interviewed as they walked along, and their worries and concerns about uranium would be broadcast over the local and national networks. One march was led by a contingent of men dressed in pinstriped suits carrying umbrellas and a large placard saying, "Uranium Pushers"; behind them huddled a group of children with simulated deformities, the "By-products of Uranium." This imaginative approach appealed to the television cameras; it illustrated the medical implications of nuclear power simply and forcefully. The scene was broadcast on every television channel that evening.

Our marches yielded many practical results. First, they educated the people in the streets; second, they drew the media, thereby educating thousands of people sitting in their homes; third, they alerted politicians to the fact that many of their constituents were opposed to uranium mining, and that they had better learn more about the subject if they wanted to be re-elected; and, finally, they produced a tremendous feeling of unity and solidarity among people from all classes of society. I always had the feeling that our marches exemplified the way people should relate to one another, as concerned human beings working together for survival.

We also organized a teach-in on the steps of Parliament House. We made banners proclaiming the medical side effects of uranium. We talked to people in the street and, if they showed concern, gave them information. Large bumper stickers were printed, reading "Uranium Is Thalidomide Forever." They were posted on cars and buildings all over town and soon were ubiquitous. We buried a time capsule containing a photo of a normal human baby under the foundations of a new highrise building, so that people could dig it up two thousand years hence to see what human beings once looked like.

We used every large gathering—whether anti-uranium or nonrelated—to solicit signatures for petitions and newspaper advertisements. We stood outside supermarkets. We canvassed churches, hospitals, schools, and universities. (I even canvassed the Australian Pediatric Association, collecting signatures from my colleagues during a cocktail hour.) The statement which these people signed read:

> The Australian Government, under pressure from local and overseas interests, has decided to mine, use, enrich, and export uranium from Australia's considerable deposits. Power plants, fueled by uranium, produce vast quantities of highly radioactive nuclear wastes for which there is no satisfactory method of disposal. Inevitable contamination of the environment will lead to an increase in birth defects, leukemia, and other malignant disease. Nuclear power plants may present as great a threat to the survival of life on earth as does nuclear war. This vital issue is above profit or politics. We call upon the leaders of our country to reject the mining of uranium for use in Australia or overseas and to bring pressure to bear on other governments to do likewise.

Everyone who signed also donated $1, and after several weeks we had two to three thousand signatures and enough money to buy one third of a page in the state newspaper. At the bottom of the advertisement we added a line inviting anyone who agreed with the statement to send us their name and donation. Within weeks we had thousands more signatures—and enough money to repeat the ad in the national newspaper.

As more and more events took place, we were befriended by many reporters who had become convinced that uranium is dangerous. They covered all our events, even though the station managers were often allied with big business and tended to be pro-uranium.

Several loose-knit organizations co-ordinated our major efforts: CANE (Campaign Against Nuclear Energy), MAUM (Movement Against Uranium Mining), and FOE (Friends of the Earth). Although we met once a week to report on what we had all been doing, there were no rules and few agendas. Each individual was totally free to do what he or she considered necessary to further the cause. The organizations imposed no constraints, recognizing that we were all driven by a sense of urgency.

Since 1976 America's antinuclear movement has grown by leaps and bounds. Small local citizens' groups are springing up all over the country and are uniting to work together. Mobilization for Survival, a new national organization, comprises antinuclear and peace groups united to fight nuclear power, eliminate nuclear weapons, stop the arms race, and use the world's resources to fund human needs. I am very excited about these new movements.

One of the high points of this new effort occurred in 1977, when New England's Clamshell Alliance occupied the site of the Seabrook, New Hampshire, nuclear power plant: 1414 people were arrested and jailed in state armories. These people are so adamantly opposed to nuclear power that they accepted not only temporary jailing but, later, sentences ranging from one to four months. This event signalled the beginning of a tough new movement in which people are prepared to fight the system that condones, legalizes, and builds death-producing industries and weapons.

I spoke during the Seabrook occupation to a large rally of people gathered at a nearby beach. Later I was called in as an "expert witness" for Carter Wentworth, the first person to be formally tried for the Seabrook occupation. The judge ruled my evidence inadmissible, even though it concerned the medical dangers of nuclear power, and these dangers had convinced Carter to occupy the site. He was appealing on the grounds of a law of competing harms, which stipulates that if the danger from the occupation was less to society than the potential danger imposed by a nuclear power plant, the defendant must be ruled innocent. Without giving any reason why, the judge determined that this law was inapplicable. I realized that day that the spread of nuclear power could not be stopped here by appealing to the legal system; only by transforming

America's concerned citizens into the political majority could the antinuclear movement hope to attain its goals.

I have testified at hearings held on nuclear power plants in Long Island and Massachusetts. Each time I found myself talking to lawyers employed by the utilities, who know little or nothing about biology. The judges in these hearings are employed by the NRC. Thus, the litigation system surrounding nuclear reactors is often farcical. Subject to obvious conflict of interest, the arbitrators cannot be impartial. I would therefore advise people who are concerned about nuclear power to pressure the legal system to behave responsibly; to mobilize in large numbers; march; demonstrate; educate and teach in schools, churches, political meetings—wherever people gather. A large movement is mobilizing against nuclear war, led by physicians, lawyers, churches, engineers, teachers, musicians, and hundreds of thousands of lay people.

We are the curators of life on earth, standing at a crossroads in time. We must awake from our false sense of security and commit ourselves to using democracy constructively to save the human species, or our democratic heritage will atrophy and be lost.

The nuclear power plants encroaching on our suburbs make it no longer possible for Americans to bury their heads in the sand and pretend that the fissioned atom does not exist: The radioactive isotopes discharged into the environment by nuclear reactors and nuclear waste are identical to those released when an atomic bomb explodes. Moreover, the spread of commercial nuclear technology to other nations guarantees the uncontrollable proliferation of nuclear weapons. Obviously, something must be done to stop this spread and achieve total nuclear disarmament, but American and Soviet politicians seem unable and/or unwilling to take appropriate action. It is therefore up to us, the people of the world. The citizens of Australia, Europe, and now the U.S.A. are mobilizing, setting a shining example that a society can effectively use its democracy for the good. Following its lead, we must all find the courage to take our destiny into our own hands.

The struggle by the antinuclear forces in the United States and other parts of the world has already begun to meet stiff resistance. In Australia, in June 1978, Prime Minister Malcolm Fraser's Liberal Government passed into law an Environmental Protection (Nuclear Activities) Act that could turn that country into a police state: empowering a government ministry to take any action considered necessary to control and eliminate hazards associated with "a situation resulting from nuclear activity," the Act gives the government virtually uncontrolled power to censor the press and detain antinuclear activists indefinitely, and without trial, whenever necessary to protect "nuclear activities." In the United States, meanwhile, some nuclear companies and utilities have already planted intelligence agents to spy on the growing opposition (a House Commerce subcommittee is investigating to see if such activities include illegal surveillance); the FBI has already begun to impugn the patriotism of antinuclear activists, alleging that their effort is an alien enemy attack on the United States. The truth is that this nation's only real enemies are the forces of disease and death.

Will we survive or will we destroy ourselves? What else matters, if we are wiped out this decade, this year, this week, this hour, or this minute? Nuclear technology is the crucial issue facing us today. To defeat that technology, we must begin now to shape world events.

The power of an aroused public is unbeatable. Vietnam and Watergate proved that. It must be demonstrated again. It is not yet too late, for while there is life there is hope. There is no cause for pessimism, for already I have seen great obstacles surmounted. Nor need we be afraid, for I have seen democracy work.

Each of us must accept total responsibility for the earth's survival. Ultimately, the future rests upon our commitment as individuals—as parents, providing a healthy and secure future for their children; as students, unwilling to accept a future of sickness and war; as citizens, believing that it is the people who should hold the balance of power in a democracy; as taxpayers, exhausted by an insane arms race and opposed to the waste of the earth's resources; as workers, farmers, professionals, artists, corporate employees, public servants, environmentalists, industrialists, rich and poor, black and white, red and yellow, men and women. In the face of nuclear technology, concern for human survival surpasses all social, political, and economic divisions. All of us—regardless of class, creed, or political affiliation—want the human race to survive. As members of the same species, we must work in harmony toward our common goal.

Epilogue: Three Mile Island

At four a.m. on March 28, 1979, the worst accident in the history of the U.S. nuclear industry began and, within several hours, the badly damaged radioactive core was thirty to sixty minutes from a meltdown. Although later engineering analysis doubted that a true "China Syndrome" could have taken place because of the hard rock foundation beneath the reactor, it is certainly well within the realm of possibility that a large fraction of the radioactive inventory could have been released into the atmosphere.

A normally operating 1000 megawatt reactor contains 15 billion curies of radiation, the equivalent of the long-lived isotopes released by the explosion of 1,000 Hiroshima bombs. When an atomic bomb explodes, much of the fallout is forced into the stratosphere and circulates west to east around the globe. Fallout is intermittent, occurring only with low pressure atmospheric conditions. However, in the case of a meltdown, any damage incurred to human population and property would depend upon the prevailing wind direction at the time of the release of the radioactive plume, and the plume would hover close to the earth depositing fallout continuously along its path. To understand the awful magnitude of destruction from a meltdown, the Government sponsored Rasmussen Report, now updated by the Union of Concerned Scientists, is very helpful. It states that in the *worst possible case* (a Class 9 Accident), if 10 million people were exposed; 3,300 people would die from severe radiation damage within several days; 10,000 to 100,000 people would develop acute radiation sickness within two to six weeks of initial exposure; 45,000 would become short of breath since the intensely radioactive gases produce lung damage; 240,000 others would develop acute hypothyroidism with symptoms of weight gain, lassitude, susceptibility to cold, impaired and slow mental functions, loss of appetite, constipation and absent menstruation; 350,000 males would become temporarily sterile as the gamma radiation would damage the sperm; 40,000 to 100,000 women would cease to menstruate, many permanently. In the fetal population, up to 100,000 babies would be born cretins with mental retardation because the radioactive iodine would destroy the thyroid gland; 1,500 others would develop microcephaly (small heads) since the developing central nervous system is highly susceptible to the deleterious effects of radiation. There would be 3,000 deaths in utero. Five to fifty years later, cancer would develop in various body organs of 270,000 people and there would be 28,800 cases of thyroid malignancy.

Economically, a meltdown would cost approximately 14 billion dollars in property damage, but even more horrifying is the fact that it could contaminate an area the size of Pennsylvania for hundreds to thousands of years making it uninhabitable.

As of 1980, 30 million Americans presently live within thirty miles of a nuclear reactor. How many could be evacuated?

At the time of Three Mile Island (TMI) the existence of an effective state by state evacuation plan was not a prerequisite for granting an operating license for a reactor. Under current regulations, individual states can submit emergency plans to the Nuclear Regulatory Commission (NRC) for approval, but at the time of the accident only a few states had NRC approved plans and Pennsylvania was not among them.

The size and location of the population to be evacuated would depend on the prevailing wind conditions, but the evacuation of a large population—New York City and surrounding areas, for instance, within hours after a meltdown—would be a frightening and utterly impossible scenario.

Even if such an evacuation were possible, physicians are totally unprepared to cope with such a large population of contaminated patients. Presently, our medical education does not include decontamination and treatment of radioactive patients; neither is the issue addressed in medical journals. Government regulations state that a patient should be hosed down to remove the isotopes from his skin and the contaminated water should then be drained. But it would be very dangerous for medical personnel to handle contaminated patients because they themselves could become contaminated. The sorrowful truth is that we cannot decontaminate radioactive lungs or other body organs, nor can we treat organs acutely damaged by radioactive exposure. We cannot cure sterility, and those males who might regain their fertility would have to be strongly advised not to reproduce since their sperm would almost certainly have sustained some genetic damage from radiation exposure. The medical community has made some progress in recent years in cancer treatment, but most forms of adult cancer are still incurable.

We know of only a few varyingly effective modes of

medical action to follow at the time of a meltdown. First of all, it is advisable that all people living within a hundred mile radius of a reactor have a supply of inert potassium iodide tablets in their medicine cabinets available for use in such an emergency. If a medically prescribed dose were taken thirty minutes to several hours before exposure, the nonradioactive iodine would be absorbed by the thyroid gland and subsequent uptake of radioactive iodine by the thyroid could be blocked. For exposed, unprotected patients who developed acute hypothyroidism, a thyroid extract could restore normal endocrine balance. A much less effective treatment for those who had no medication available could be to take a laxative immediately. By reducing transit time through the gut, absorption of the radioactive isotopes could be impeded. In short, we are hardly prepared to face such an emergency.

How did TMI happen at all?

It began with a mechanical failure and automatic shutdown of the main feedwater pumps in the secondary coolant system which closed some valves, thereby causing the water in the primary coolant system covering the radioactive core to quickly heat and expand. The pressurizer operator relief valves (PORV) in the primary system automatically opened as designed to do and started draining precious cooling water away from the core. When that happened, the reactor scrammed—control rods automatically dropped between the uranium fuel rods in the core, stopping the fission reaction. The core, however, remained exceedingly hot and the light on the operating panel failed to indicate that the valves were not shut but stuck open. The valves remained open for approximately two hours before the operators understood the situation. Thinking the core was covered with water, the operators turned off the water flow from the emergency cooling system causing the water to rapidly drain from the core; through the PORV while the emergency cooling system was closed tight.

Then, the one hundred tons of uranium core overheated and the zirconium cladding of the rods reacted with water at 2,200° F, melted and exposed the cooling water to highly radioactive fission products and alpha emittors. The core was severely damaged, and the hydrogen gas which was produced by a zirconium-water chemical reaction, collected in the containment vessel, and spontaneously exploded several hours after the accident thus began, exposing the containment vessel to dangerous explosive forces that could have weakened it. Believe it or not, this incredibly serious event was not recognized by either the operators, the utility or the NRC for several days. As more hydrogen continued to be generated over following days, Chairman Hendrie of the NRC and others feared that oxygen released by radiolysis from water molecules would unite with the hydrogen bubble, explode and possibly rupture the containment vessel releasing large quantities of radiation; or else the noncondensible hydrogen bubble would eventually uncover the core leading to a meltdown. Meanwhile, in order to reassure the American people that the reactor posed no danger, President and Mrs. Carter were taken into the operating room of the TMI unit 2 on the afternoon of April 1 at the height of the anxiety about this hydrogen bubble. This foolish exercise exposed the President to unnecessary danger.

Throughout the accident, the highly radioactive cooling water was being pumped through the PORV onto the floor of the reactor and from there into a tank in an adjacent auxiliary building. At this time, large quantities of radioactive gases were vented from this auxiliary tank from a leaking valve into the atmosphere, so intermittent plumes of radioactivity were dispersed from the reactor. The wind blew mainly to the northwest quadrant. The radiation was measured by various gamma counting devices. Beta and Alpha radiation were not measured, but it has been estimated that 2.4 to 13 million curies of noble gases—xenon and krypton—were released, and 13-17 curies of radioactive iodine escaped. Although noble gases do not combine chemically in the body, they are absorbed by the lungs after inhalation. Ten times more fat soluble than water soluble, they tend to concentrate in the abdominal fat pad and the fat of the upper thighs. Xenon 133 and Krypton 85 are high energy gamma emittors like X-rays. Thus, the reproductive organs of people living near TMI could well have been exposed to gamma radiation, particularly if they were immersed in clouds of noble gases.

Because the monitoring device in the auxiliary building stack went off scale early in the accident (it was not designed to measure such large quantities of radiation), estimates of radiation release were extrapolated from radiation monitors some distance from the stack. Therefore, no hard data exists concerning the absolute quantities of the radiation release. Furthermore, because Alpha and Beta radiation was not routinely measured, it is impossible to precisely know which radioactive elements escaped. Noble gas measurements were not begun until April 5—eight days after the accident began. In other words, all calculations are only educated guesses from the available but inadequate data.

Official estimations from the government-sponsored Kemmeny Commission also predict that less than one case of cancer will occur from the radioactive releases in the exposed population during their lifetimes. However, using the Hanford-Mancuso data for cancer incidence, 60-70 deaths from cancer are a possible figure.

The facts are: Nobody knows precisely where the plumes blew, whether the radioactivity touched the ground or how it was dispersed. We do know, though, that the radioactive plume was monitored 250 miles away from the plant.

Dose calculations were made by averaging the radiation dose over the totally exposed population, but some people could well have been exposed to higher doses than others because of the uneven distribution of the radioactive gaseous plume and the fact that the population is not homogeneous. The dose to the adult thyroid of Iodine 131 was calculated to be

11.1 millirems, but the dose to the fetal thyroid would be ten to twenty times greater, and fetuses are many times more sensitive to the mutagenic effects of radiation than adults. Also, the carcinogenic effects of radioisotopes react synergistically with other carcinogens in the body to promote cancer. Therefore, depending ing upon the state of the environment, there very well could be an increase in various forms of cancer in the TMI area.

Dr. Gordon MacLeod, former Secretary of Health in Pennsylvania, was sworn in to his position twelve days before the accident. Out of town at the time of the accident, he was told about the radiation release by phone. He asked for someone in the State Health Department who knew all about the health effects of radiation release to phone him. There was no such person. He then asked for the liaison to the Bureau of Radiation Protection to call him. Again, no such person. He then requested that books on the subject be collected from the State Health Department Library so he could investigate them in the morning. There were no such books because there was no library. Subsequently, Dr. MacLeod initiated medical follow-up studies of the exposed population. He was also concerned about the medical consequences of the clean-up. In fact, the Kemmeny report states that the accident at TMI has just begun. It will take four to five years to complete.

The one million gallons of highly radioactive water that spilled onto the floor of the reactor buildings as well as the large volumes of radioactive gas and the mess of collapsed and fragmented hot fuel rods will all have to be removed from the reactor site. Not only is this operation expected to take years, but it will invariably involve more contamination for nuclear workers as well as the release of more radioactivity into the Harrisburg environment.

Dr. MacLeod requested that the Department of Health be intimately involved in this clean-up, but as this story becomes more and more surreal, he was fired, or as the official word came through the media, he was "requested to resign." Several people from the Pennsylvania Department of Health have since resigned and the only two departments now in charge of the operation are the Bureau of Radiation Protection and the Governor's office. There are no physicians supervising or monitoring the clean-up.

A number of possible health consequences of the nuclear power industry have been and still are largely ignored by the NRC. Their internal report, known as the Rogovin Report, states, "the NRC has provided neither leadership nor management of the nation's safety program for commercial plants." In fact, early in the accident, former Chairman of the NRC Joseph Hendrie said, "We are operating almost totally in the blind, his (Governor Thornburgh's) information is ambiguous, mine is non-existent, and—I don't know—it's like a couple of blind men staggering around making decisions."

On another occasion, Harold Denton, who was the appointed spokesman for President Carter, said, "Yes, I think the important thing for evacuation to get ahead of the plume is to get a start, rather than sitting here to wait to die. Even if we can't minimize the individual dose, there might still be a chance to limit the population dose." But throughout the accident, as evacuation plans were being discussed by the NRC, the radioactive plume had already moved over the population.

When Governor Thornburgh asked Chairman Hendrie, "Is there anyone in the country who has experience with the health consequences of such a release?" he replied, "Ah—not in the sense that it's been studied and understood in any real way. There were back in the days when they were doing bomb testing. They managed to give groups of soldiers and occasionally a few civilians doses in the low rem range —a subject of discussion these days, but that's about the only comparable experience that occurs to me. You are talking now about a major release, not about the small ones that have occurred thus far."

The presidentially appointed Kemmeny Commission Report (October 1979) and the Rogovin Report (January 1980) both say that the state of the nuclear industry at the time of the accident was one of chaos. Accidents like TMI had almost happened twice before: once in 1974 at a Westinghouse reactor in Switzerland; and in 1977 at Toledo Edison's Davis Besse plant in Ohio. Both involved the failed PORV valve and misleading indications from the control panel which erroneously indicated the reactor coolant system was full of water.

A brief account of the Swiss accident was submitted to the NRC, but it did not prompt notification to operators that they might be misled by their instruments if a valve stuck open. The Davis Besse accident was intensely analyzed by the NRC, and then was filed away and never circulated.

Unfortunately, none of this is unique. The NRC receives many such reports, some trivial, some important, but in either case, the information is not systematically reviewed. For the most part, these reports are summarized in a few sentences for computer listing, distributed haphazardly to various staff offices and then simply filed away. Furthermore, there is absolutely no institutional mechanism within the NRC for developing solutions to potential dangers and insuring that such solutions are integrated into reactor operations through design changes, new procedures or improved training.

The Rogovin Report states: "We have found in the NRC an organization that is not so much badly managed as it is not managed at all. In our opinion, the Commission is incapable, in its present configuration, of managing a comprehensive national safety program for existing nuclear power plants adequate to insure public health and safety."

There are five NRC Commissioners, working ineffectively together. Most of their meetings are spent discussing isolated safety issues, personnel, budget matters, administrative chores and export licensing—very little time is spent deliberating the crucial issues relating to reactor safety. This general inefficiency filters down to the NRC staff, where one of the most glaring deficiencies is a lack of any program requiring members to acquire experience in the design, construction and operation of nuclear reactors as well as radiation detection. In fact, Chairman Hendrie was the only NRC Commissioner with expertise in reactor engineering. Nor is the staff directly supervised on a daily basis by the Commission. They aren't even housed in the same state! The Commissioners and their staffs work in downtown Washington, D.C., while the NRC general staff are scattered among six office buildings in suburban Maryland. To make matters even worse, a strong we/they attitude has developed on both sides. To further illustrate what a potentially devastating mindset is operable there, before TMI, both the nuclear industry and the NRC had the attitude that such an accident was not *a credible event* and therefore *would never occur*.

The unfortunate truth is that nuclear operators are trained for only normal power operations and for the start-up and shut-down of the plant, not for the advent of accidents. The area of operating training has been a "backwater" with most utilities as well as the NRC.

The Rogovin Report says that the problems revealed at TMI—inadequate training, unreasonably scanty manning sessions, lack of any requirements for minimum on-site technical supervisory competence—are common to many and probably most power plants.

The point is that NRC inspectors spend a great deal of their time confirming utility personnel's bookkeeping procedures for maintenance and the logging in of any operating problems. One operator wrote, after experiencing a severe potential accident in the control room of TMI Unit 2 one year earlier, "You might do well to remember this is only the tip of the iceberg. Incidents like this are easy to get into and the best operators in the world can't compensate for multiple casualties which are complicated by mechanical and control failure." The President's Commission found that the NRC failed to recognize that human beings who manage and operate reactors constitute an important safety system. And during the accident itself, the NRC was reluctant and did not assume control of the crippled plant. They only monitored and advised because the philosophy in the industry is, "the licensee is in charge even when they are incompetent."

The Rogovin Report also found *a wide spectrum in the capability of the various nuclear utilities to operate existing plants in a safe fashion.*

Although current law places sole responsibility for the safe construction and operation of nuclear plants on the utilities, typically, the utilities possess less nuclear expertise than the architectural/engineering firms who design and build the reactors and even the NRC. After the licensing process is obtained by the firms and the NRC and the plant goes into service—the utility is on its own. Rogovin thinks that some utilities will, in fact, be unable to afford the increased safety requirements, competent site management or first class trained operators necessary in the wake of TMI investigations.

But despite the most damning reports of the entire nuclear industry and the NRC, the Rogovin Report and the Kemmeny Commission did not recommend the closing of any presently operating reactors. Why were they compromised? And must we wait for the inevitable meltdown before any further action is taken? If this country, and along with it the rest of the world, continues to rely more and more on nuclear power, a meltdown disaster is almost predictable, and when it does occur, disaster and chaos from the medical and psychological effects as well as the shutdown of electricity from all nuclear power plants will be the result.

For years now, the utilities and nuclear power industry have refused to listen to scientific logic and reasoning concerning the dangers of this technology.

In the light of past accidents and all the events surrounding TMI, perhaps it is time for emotion and for passion and for commitment to stir our souls and our hearts and our minds once again into action.

Bibliography

BOOKS

Alexander, Peter, *Atomic Radiation and Life*. New York, Penguin Books, 1965.

Aronow, Saul, Ervin, Frank R., M.D., and Sidel, Victor, W., M.D., eds., *The Fallen Sky: Medical Consequences of Thermonuclear War*. New York, Hill and Wang, 1963.

Asimov, Isaac, *A Short History of Chemistry*. New York, Doubleday, 1965.

Berger, John, *Nuclear Power: The Unviable Option*. Palo Alto, California, Ramparts Press, 1976.

Commoner, Barry, *Poverty of Power*. New York, Alfred Knopf, 1976.

Copeland, Lewis, and Lamm, Lawrence W., eds., *The World's Great Speeches*. New York, Dover Publications, 1973.

DeGroot, Lesley J., ed., et al., *Radiation-Associated Thyroid Carcinoma*. New York, Grune & Stratton, 1977.

Faulkner, Peter, ed., *The Silent Bomb: A Guide to the Nuclear Energy Controversy*. New York, Vintage Books, 1977.

Gofman, John W., and Tamplin, Arthur R., *Poisoned Power*. Emmaus, Pa., Rodale Press, 1971.

Gyorgy, Anna, et al., *No Nukes: Everyone's Guide to Nuclear Power*. Boston, South End Press, 1978.

Lewin, Leonard C., ed., *Report from Iron Mountain on the Possibility and Desirability of Peace*. New York, Dial Press, 1967.

Lifton, Robert Jay, *Death in Life*. New York, Random House, 1967.

Nader, Ralph and Abbotts, John, *The Menace of Atomic Energy*. New York, W. W. Norton & Co., Inc., 1977.

Nuclear Power, Issues and Choices. Report of the Nuclear Energy Policy Study Group. Ballinger Publishing Co., 1977.

Olson, McKinley C., *Unacceptable Risk*. New York, Bantam Books, 1976.

Patterson, Walter C., *Nuclear Power*. New York, Penguin Books, 1976.

Pauling, Linus, *No More War*. New York, Dodd, Mead and Co., 1958.

Pizzarello, Donald J., Ph.D., and Witcofski, Richard L., Ph.D.,

Basic Radiation Biology. Philadelphia, Lea and Febiger, 1975.

Russell, Bertrand, *The Autobiography of Bertrand Russell.* London, George Allen and Unwin Ltd., Vol. I–IV., 1971.

Stockholm Internation Peace Research Institute, *Weapons of Mass Destruction and the Environment.* London, Taylor and Francis Ltd., 1977.

Union of Concerned Scientists, *The Nuclear Fuel Cycle: A Survey of the Public Health, Environmental, and National Security Effects of Nuclear Power.* Cambridge, The MIT Press, 1975.

PERIODICALS

Abbotts, John, and McCarthy, Mary, "What's wrong with the Atomic Industry?" Public Interest Research Group (PIRG), July 1977.

Alfven, H., "Energy and Environment." The Bulletin of the Atomic Scientists, pp. 5–7, May 1972.

Anderson, Jack, "Colorado Plant Eyed as Radiation Source." Washington Post, March 25, 1978.

Anson, Robert Sam, "The Neutron Bomb." New Times, pp. 24–32, August 5, 1977.

Archer, U.E., Wagoner, J.K., and Lundin, F.E., "Lung Cancer Among Uranium Miners in the United States." Health Physics, Vol. 25, pp. 351–371, 1973.

"A-Tests May Have Exposed 300,000." Washington Post, February 11, 1978.

"A-Test Veterans In Area Should Call 295-0586." Washington Post, February 11, 1978.

"Atom-Job Transfers Tied To Drugs And Alcohol." UPI, The New York Times, August 8, 1977.

Bair, W.J., and Thompson, R.C., "Plutonium: Biomedical Research." Science, Vol. 183, pp. 715–722, February 1974.

Barnaby, Frank, "The Mounting Prospects of Nuclear War." A Report of the Stockholm International Peace Research Institute. The Bulletin of the Atomic Scientists, Vol. 33, pp. 10–21, June 1977.

Barnet, Richard, "A Time to Stop." Sojourners, Vol. 7, March 1978.

―――. "Less Big Power Tension, Greater War Danger." New York Times, December 28, 1977.

Baverstock, K.F., and Vennart, J., "Emergency Reference Levels for Reactor Accidents: A Re-Examination of the Windscale Reactor Accident." Health Physics, Vol. 30, pp. 339–344, April 1976.

Beirwaltes, W.H., et. al., "Radioactive Iodine Concentration In The Fetal Human Thyroid Gland From Fallout." The

107

Journal of the American Medical Association, August 27, 1960, Vol. 173, pp. 1895–1902.

Benedict, Howard, "An Arms Race In Space." Boston Sunday Globe, March 19, 1978.

Bertell, Rosalie, Ph.D., G.N.S.H., "The Nuclear Worker and Ionizing Radiation." Banquet Address before Meeting of the American Industrial Hygiene Association, May 9, 1977.

Bjella, Lanceford C. Notes of testimony before Colorado Department of Health officials, Denver, Colorado.

Breitenstein, B.D., Jr., M.D., Norwood, W.D., M.D., and Newton, Jr., C.E. United States Transuranium Registry. Annual Report October 1, 1975 to October 1, 1976 To ERDA Division of Biomedical and Environmental Research. Hanford Environmental Health Foundation, Richland, Washington, December 1976.

Bross, Irwin, D.J., Ph.D., and Natarajan, N., M.S., "Leukemia from Low-Level Radiation—Identification of Susceptible Children." New England Journal of Medicine, July 20, 1972.

Burnham, David, "Nuclear Plant Got U.S. Contracts Despite Many Security Violations." New York Times, July 4, 1977.

———. "Panel Hints Nuclear Electricity May Be Costly." New York Times, April 11, 1978.

———. "U.S. Commission Blocks Shipment of Uranium for India Power Plants." New York Times, April 21, 1978.

———. "Congress Unit Says U.S. Tried to Balk California Nuclear Curbs." New York Times, January 16, 1978.

———. "A Student's Bomb Design Prompts Call for More Nuclear Safeguards." New York Times, March 23, 1978.

———. "Ex-C.I.A. Man Says Johnson Heard in '68 Israel Had A-Bombs." New York Times, March 2, 1978.

Burt, Richard, "U.S. Analysis Doubts There Can Be Victor In Major Atomic War." New York Times, January 6, 1978.

———. "Pentagon Reviewing Nuclear War Plans." New York Times, December 16, 1977.

———. "Neutron Bomb Study Irks Pentagon Aides." New York Times, February 1, 1978.

Cairnes, John, "The Cancer Problem." Scientific American, pp. 64–78, November 1975.

Campbell, E.E., Milligan, M.F., Moss, W.D., Schultz, H.F., and McInray, J., "Plutonium in Autopsy Tissue." Los Alamos Scientific Laboratory Report, L.A. 4875, 1973.

Clayton, Bruce Douglas, "Planning for the Day After Doomsday." The Bulletin of the Atomic Scientists, Vol. 33, pp. 49–53, September 1977.

Cobb, John C., M.D., M.P.H., ed., "Surprising Findings About Plutonium Dangers to Man Reported at the International Atomic Energy Meeting in San Francisco, California," December 25, 1975.

Cockburn, Andrew, "The Nuclear Disaster They Didn't Want To Tell You About." Esquire, Vol. 89, pp. 39–43, April 25, 1978.

Cohen, Bernard L., "The Hazards in Plutonium Dispersal." Institute for Energy Analysis, March 1975.

Comey, D.D., "The Legacy of Uranium Tailings." The Bulletin of the Atomic Scientists, pp. 43–45, September 1975.

Conrad, Robert A., M.D., et al., "A Twenty-Year Review of Medical Findings in a Marshallese Population Accidentally Exposed to Radioactive Fallout." Brookhaven National Laboratory, Associated Universities, Inc. USERDA.

Cooke, Robert, and Dietz, Jean, "Energy Future Lies In the Solar Cell." Boston Globe, April 29, 1978.

Cubie, Jim, "The Unacceptable Risks of Nuclear Energy: The Link Between Your Light Switch and the Bomb." Sojourners, Vol. 7, March 1978.

Cutler, S.J., Meyers, M.H., and Green, S.B., "Trends in Survival Rates In Patients with Cancer." New England Journal of Medicine, Vol. 293, pp. 122–124, 1975.

deVilliers, A.J., and Windish, J.P., "Lung Cancer in Flurospar Mining Community." British Journal of Industrial Medicine, 21, pp. 96–109, 1964.

Diethorn, W.S., and Stockho, W.L., "The Dose to Man From Atmospheric ^{85}Kr." Health Physics, Vol. 23, pp. 653–662, November 1972.

Dietz, Jean, "Scientists Unveil N-Waste Proposal." Boston Globe, March 4, 1978.

Eason, Charles F., M.D., "Medical Exposures of Radiation Workers—Should They Be Recorded?" Journal of Occupational Medicine, Vol. 16, March 1974.

Edsall, John T., "Toxicity of Plutonium and some other actinides," Bulletin of the Atomic Scientists, pp. 27–37, September 1976.

Eisenbud, M., "Radioactivity In The Environment: State of Radioactivity In The Environment." Pediatrics, Vol. 41, No. 1, Part II, January, 1968, pp. 174–193.

Fialka, John J., "Did Atom Agencies Squelch Report on Cancer Risk?" Washington Star, January 19, 1978.

"Fifteen Nations Agree on N-Safeguards." Globe Wire Services, Boston Evening Globe, January 12, 1978.

Ford, Daniel F., "Nuclear Power: Some Basic Economic Issues." Union of Concerned Scientists, April 28, 1975.

———. "A History of Federal Nuclear Safety Assessments: From WASH 2740 Through the Reactor Safety Study." Union of Concerned Scientists, 1977.

———. Kendall, Henry W., and Tye, Lawrence S., "Browns Ferry, The Regulatory Failure." Union of Concerned Scientists, June 10, 1976.

"Fourteen Cases of Cancer at Weapon Research Lab Studied."
New York Times, January 25, 1978.

Fox, R.W., Kellener, G.G., and Kerr, C.B., "Ranger Uranium
Inquiry, First Report." Australian Government Publishing
Service, Camberra, October 28, 1976.

Gillette, Robert, "Transient Nuclear Workers: A Special Case
for Standards." Science, Vol. 16, October 1974.

———. "Study on Nuclear Radiation Sparks Health Controversy." Los Angeles Times, December 3, 1977.

Glasstone, Samuel, ed., "The Effects of Nuclear Weapons."
United States Department of Defense, U.S. Atomic Energy
Commission, pp. 587–625, February 1964.

Gofman, John W., M.D., "The Fission-Product Equivalence
Between Nuclear Reactors and Nuclear Weapons." Senate
Congressional Record, Proceedings and Debates of the 92nd
Congress, 1st Session, Vol. 117, July 8, 1971.

———. "The Cancer Hazard from Inhaled Plutonium." Committee for Nuclear Responsibility, CNR Report 1975–IR,
Dublin, California, May 14, 1975.

———. "Estimated Production of Human Lung Cancers By
Plutonium from Worldwide Fallout." Committee for Nuclear Responsibility, San Francisco, California, July 10,
1975.

———. "The Plutonium Controversy." Reprint Journal of
American Medical Association, Vol. 236, July 19, 1976.

———. Statement on lung cancer hazards of Pu-239 and
Americium-241. Pamphlet, Women Strike for Peace, Washington, D.C., February 21, 1978.

Gorman, J., "Wandering in the Nuclear Wasteland." The
Sciences, pp. 6–10, November 1975.

Gottstein, Klaus, "Nuclear Energy for the Third World." The
Bulletin of the Atomic Scientists, Vol. 33, pp. 44–48, June
1977.

Gwyne, Peter, "Plutonium: 'free' fuel or invitation to a
catastrophe." Smithsonian.

Gyorgi, Anna, "Nuclear Waste Storage." New Age, June
1975.

"Hardsell on Nuclear Safety." Editorial, New York Times,
March 2, 1978.

Hart, J.C., Ritchie, R.H., and Varnadore, Beverly S., eds.,
"Population Exposures." Proceedings of the 8th Midyear
Topical Symposium of the Health Physics Society, Knox-
ville, Tennessee, October 21–24, 1974.

"Health Expert Says U.S. Should Reduce Radiation Exposure."
New York Times, January 25, 1978.

"Hot Town." Environment section, Time, p. 50, December
20, 1971.

House, Karen Elliott, "U.S. is Facing Problem of How to

Dismantle Used Nuclear Reactors." Wall Street Journal, October 12, 1977.

Ibrahim, Youssef M., "U.S. Nuclear Industry Sees Bill a Threat to Exports." New York Times, February 15, 1978.

Ibser, H.W., "The Nuclear Energy Game: Genetic Roulette." The Progressive, January 1976.

Jacobs, Paul, "Precautions Are Being Taken By Those Who Know. An Inquiry Into the Power and Responsibilities of the AEC." The Atlantic, pp. 45–56, February 1971.

Johnson, E.R., and McBride, J.A., "The Plutonium Problem." INFO, Atomic Industrial Forum Public Affairs and Info Program. Presented at Workshop "The Nuclear Controversy in the U.S.A.," Lucerne, Switzerland, May 1974.

Kistiakowski, George B., "Can the Arms Race be Curbed?" Boston Sunday Globe, April 16, 1978.

Klurfeld, Jim, "A Very Private Public Man." Boston Sunday Globe, April 23, 1978.

Kneese, A.V., "The Faustian Bargain." Resources, pp. 1–5, September 1973.

Kochupillai, N., Verma, I.C., Grewai, M.S., Ramalinga Swami V., "Down's Syndrome and Related Abnormalities in an Area of High Background Radiation in Coastal Kerala." Nature, Vol. 262, July 1, 1976.

Kohn, Howard. "The Nuclear Industry's Terrible Power and How It Silenced Karen Silkwood." Rolling Stone, March 27, 1975.

———. "The Government's Quiet War on Scientists Who Know Too Much." Rolling Stone, pp. 42–44, March 23, 1978.

Krey, P.W., Bogen, D., and French, E., "Plutonium in Man and His Environment." Nature, pp. 263–265, July 21, 1962.

Kunz, E., Sevc, J., and Placek, V., "Lung Cancer in Uranium Miners and Long-Term Exposure to Radon Daughter Products." Health Institute of Uranium Industry, Institute of Industrial Hygiene in Uranium Industry.

Lamb, David, "Africa's Hunger for Weapons." Los Angeles Times reprinted in Boston Globe, March 21, 1978.

Langham, W.H., "Biological Implications of the Transuranium Elements for Man." Health Physics, Vol. 22, pp. 943–952, 1972.

Lash, Terry R., Bryson, John E., and Cotton, Richard, Citizens Guide: "The National Debate on the Handling of Radioactive Wastes from Nuclear Power Plants." Natural Resources Defense Council, Inc., November 1975.

Legator, Marvin S., and Hollander, Alexander, "Occupational Monitoring of Genetic Hazards." Annals of the New York Academy of Sciences, Vol. 269, December 31, 1975.

111

Lindsey, Robert, "Domestic Arms Race Pits Livermore vs. Los Alamos." New York Times, July 31, 1977.

Lisco, H., Finkel, M.P., and Brues, A.M., "Carcinogenic Properties of Radioactive Fission Products and of Plutonium." Radiology, Vol. 49, p. 361, 1947.

Loed, Vernon. "Pennsylvania Health Chief Leaves As He Began—Swiftly." Philadelphia Inquirer, November 1, 1979.

Lyons, Richard D., "Soviet Spy Satellite with Atomic Reactor Breaks Up In Canada." New York Times, January 25, 1978.

MacNeil/Lehrer Report. Transcript of "Danger: Radiation." Educational Broadcasting Corporation and GWETA, November 25, 1977.

Magno, Paul J., Reavey, Thomas C., and Apidianakis, John C., "Iodine-129 In the Environment Around a Nuclear Fuel Reprocessing Plant." (West Valley, N.Y.) US Environmental Protection Agency, Office of Radiation Programs, Field Operation Division, Washington, D.C., October 1972.

Mancuso, Thomas F., M.D., "Study of the Lifetime Health and Mortality Experience of Employees of ERDA Contractors." Department of Industrial Environmental Health Sciences, Graduate School of Public Health, University of Pittsburgh, Penn., September 30, 1977.

Mancuso, Thomas F., M.D., Stewart Alice, M.D., and Kneale, George, M.A., "Radiation Exposures of Hanford Workers Dying From Various Causes." Proceedings of Papers presented at Meeting of 10th Midyear Topical Symposium of the Health Physics Society, N.E., New York Chapter, October 11–13, 1976 at Saratoga Springs, New York.

Martell, Edward A., "Iodine-131 Fallout from Underground Tests II." Science, Vol. 148, June 25, 1965.

———. "Actinides in the Environment and Their Uptake By Man." National Center for Atmospheric Research (NCAR), Boulder, Colorado, May 1975.

———. "Tobacco Radioactivity and Cancer in Smokers." American Scientists, Vol. 63, July–August 1975.

———. "Cesium-137 From the Environment to Man: "Metabolism and Dose." National Council on Radiation Protection and Measurements, NCRP Report No. 52, Washington, D.C.

———. "Basic Considerations in the Assessment of the Cancer Risks and Standard for Internal Alpha Emitters." Statement at public hearing on Plutonium standards sponsored by USEPA, Denver, Colorado, January 10, 1975.

McGovern, George, "The Russians Are Coming—Again." The Progressive, Vol. 41, pp. 17–23, May 1977.

McGrory, Mary, "Nuclear Energy Use Looms As Campaign Issue for Carter." Boston Globe, March 2, 1978.

Middleton, Drew, "U.S. Military Study Adds Fuel to Debate on Arms Treaty." New York Times, January 11, 1978.

————. "Soviet Is Said to Top U.S. in Military Investment." Boston Globe, January 26, 1977.

Miettinen, Jorma K., "Enhanced Radiation Warfare." The Bulletin of the Atomic Scientists, Vol. 33, pp. 32–37, September 1977.

Miller, James Nathan, "The Burning Question of Browns Ferry." The Readers Digest, pp. 103–108, April 1976.

Morgan, Karl Z., Ph.D., "Reducing Medical Exposure to Ionizing Radiation." American Industrial Hygiene Association Journal, May 1975.

————. "Suggested Reduction of Permissible Exposure to Plutonium and other Transuranium Elements." American Industrial Hygiene Association Journal, August 1975.

————. "Yes, is the Answer to Question of R.H. Thomas and D.D. Busick Is It Really Necessary to Reduce Patient Exposure?" American Industrial Hygiene Association Journal, November 1976.

————. "The Dilemma of Present Nuclear Power Programs." Presented at Hearings Before the Energy Resources Conservation and Development Commission, Sacramento, California, February 1, 1977.

NAS Beir Report, "The Effects on Populations of Exposure to Low Levels of Ionizing Radiation." Report of the National Academy of Sciences, National Research Council Committee on the Biological Effects of Ionizing Radiation, Washington, D.C., November 1972.

Natarajan, N., and Bross, Irwin, D.J., "Preconception Radiation and Leukemia." Journal of Medicine, 1973.

Northrup, John, "U.S. Suppressing Radiation Cancer Data, Environmentalists Say." Birmingham Post-Herald, November 29, 1977.

Norwood, W.D., and Newton, Jr., C.E., "U.S. Transuranium Registry Study of Thirty Autopsies." Health Physics, Vol. 28, pp. 669–675, 1975.

"Nuclear Energy's Dilemma—Disposing of Hazardous Radioactive Waste Safely." Report to Congress by the Comptroller General of the United States, GAO-Government Accounting Office, September 9, 1977.

"Nuclear Plants Are Dying." Myers' Finance and Energy, No. 255, November 4, 1977.

"Nuclear Power Costs." Twenty-Third Report by the Committee on Government Operation together with Additional, Minority, and Dissenting Views. 95th Congress, 2d Session, House Report No. 95–1090. April 26, 1978. U.S. Government Printing Office, Washington, D.C.: 1978.

"Nuclear Power Growth 1974–2000. U.S. Atomic Energy

Commission, WASH 1139 (1974), ERDA-486, Vol. 1, July 1975.

"Nuclear Waste Disposal Costs (West Valley, N.Y.)." Hearings Before a Subcommittee of the Committee on Government Operations. House of Representatives, 95th Congress, 1st Session, March 8 and 10, 1977. U.S. Government Printing Office, Washington, D.C., 1977.

O'Farrell, T.P., and Gilbert, R.O., "Transport of Radioactive Materials by Jackrabbits on the Hanford Reservation." Health Physics, Vol. 29, pp. 9–15, July 1975.

O'Toole, Thomas, "U.S. Studying N-Plant Security." Washington Post, Reprinted in Boston Globe, January 15, 1976.

Oveharenro, E.P., "An Experimental Evaluation of the Effects of Transuranium Elements on Reproductive Ability." Health Physics, 1972.

"Papers From Reactor Study in 1965 To Update WASH-740," USAEC, Brookhaven National Laboratory. On file in U.S. Nuclear Regulatory Commission Public Document Room, USAEC Press Release R-252 and Attachments, released to the public, June 1973.

Patterson, Rachelle, "N-Workers Safe but Let's Make Sure—Rickover." Boston Globe, March 1, 1978.

Pincus, Walter, "House Panel Told That Exposure Limit for Radiation Is 10 Times Too High." Washington Post, February 9, 1978.

————. "GI's Win Some Illness Claims From A-Tests." Washington Post, February 5, 1978.

————. "Dispute Arises on Who Will Run U.S. Study of '57 A-Test Effect." Washington Post, January 6, 1978.

————. "The U.S. Errs; Bikini Island Still Isn't Safe." Washington Post, March 19, 1978.

————. "Thyroid Cases from '54 H-Test Increase." Washington Post, March 27, 1978.

————. "Indecision on Neutron Bomb." Washington Post, Reprint in Boston Globe, April 5, 1978.

Polhemus, Donald W., M.D., and Koch, Richard, M.D., "Leukemia and Medical Radiation." Pediatrics, March 1959.

Pollock, Richard, "The Price Anderson Act." Critical Mass Journal, Vol. 3, pp. 3–4, January 1978.

————. "Soviets Experience Nuclear Accident." Critical Mass Journal, January 1978.

"Preliminary Notification of Event or Universal Occurrence—PNO-79-67AE" Prepared for The Nuclear Regulatory Commission at the time of Three Mile Island accident.

"Prospects for Further Proliferation of Nuclear Weapons," Central Intelligence Agency Memorandum, DC1 N10 1945/74, September 4, 1974.

"Reactor Safety Study—An Assessment of Risks in U.S. Commercial Power Plants." U.S. Nuclear Regulatory Commission, Washington, D.C., WASH-1400 (NUREG 75-014), October, 1975.

"Record Keeping Requirements Under the Occupational Safety and Health Act of 1970." U.S. Department of Labor, Occupational Safety and Health Administration, Revised 1975.

Rogovin, Mitchell and Frampton, Jr., George T. "Three Mile Island, A Report To The Commissioners and To the Public," Nuclear Regulatory Commission Special Inquiry Group, Vol. I, January, 1980.

"Report of the President's Commission on the Accident at Three Mile Island, The Need for Change: The Legacy at Three Mile Island," Washington, D.C. (Library of Congress Catalogue Card Number 79-25694), October, 1979.

"Representative Warns Village of Hazard in Nuclear Waste Plant." (West Valley, N.Y.) New York Times, March 19, 1978.

Richards, Bill, "Army In Maze Finding Nuclear Test Participants." Washington Post, February 15, 1978.

Richmond, C.R., and Thomas, R.L., "Plutonium In Man And His Environment." Nature, pp. 263–265, July 21, 1962.

Rose, D.J., "Nuclear Electric Power." Science, pp. 351–359, April 19, 1974.

Rosenbaum, Ron, "The Subterranean World of the Bomb." Harper's, Vol. 256, pp. 85–105, March 1978.

Ryer, Flo H., "The New Health and Safety Act As It Relates To Occupational Radiation Exposure." Health Physics, 1975.

Sauve, Frances, "Council Requests Study of Smoke Detectors." Washington Post, February 23, 1978.

Schadewald, Bill, "The bull market . . . Federal Government Spending by Function." Houston Business Journal, November 14, 1977.

Seldin, Charles, "Army Veteran of A-Bomb Test Dies of Leukemia." The Washington Post, February 10, 1978.

Severo, Richard, "Too Hot to Handle." New York Times Magazine, April 10, 1977.

Sikov, M.R., and Mahlum, D.D., "Plutonium In the Developing Animal." Health Physics, Vol. 22, pp. 707–712, 1972.

Sivard, Ruth Leger, "World Military and Social Expenditures 1977." WMSE Publications, 1977.

Smith, D.D., and Black, S.C., "Actinide Concentrations in Tissues from Cattle Grazing Near the Rocky Flats Plant." National Environmental Research Center Report, NERC-LV-539-36, pp. 1–33.

Smothers, Ronald, "Con Ed Welders Fear A-Plant Job, But Company Says Work or Quit." New York Times, March 24, 1978.

Solo, Pam, "Nuclear Crossroads at Rocky Flats." Sojourners, Vol. 7, March 1978.

"Soviets to US in '69: Let's Attack China." Washington Post, Reprint in Boston Globe, February 17, 1978.

Sternglass, Ernest J., Ph.D., "Strontium-90 Levels in the Milk and Diet Near Connecticut Nuclear Power Plants." October 27, 1977.

————. "Cancer Mortality Changes Around Nuclear Facilities in Connecticut." Testimony Presented at a Congressional Seminar on Low-Level Radiation, Washington, D.C., February 10, 1978.

Sullivan, Walter, "U.S. Space Mishaps In '64 and '70 Noted." New York Times, January 25, 1978.

"United States of America Nuclear Regulatory Commission, NRC/Response Center Discussion Related to Metropolitan Edison Company, Three Mile Island Station." This transcript was prepared from a tape recording.

"U.S. District Court Judge McMillan's Declaration, The Price Anderson Act Unconstitutional," Carolina Environmental Study Group, Charlotte, N.C., March 31, 1977.

Waldrop, Mitch, "The Technology Behind Nuclear Proliferation." C&EN, Washington, D.C., pp. 17–23, July 25, 1977.

Walker, Greg, "The Nuclear Playground." The Australian, No. 3830, November 9, 1976.

Wasserbach, Anna E., "Where to Throw Away a Radioactive Swab?" (letter to the editor) Woodstock Times, February 9, 1978.

Weighart, James, "The Dangers Aloft: A Matter of Relativity." Boston Globe, January 26, 1978.

Weinberg, A.M., "Social Institutions and Nuclear Energy." Science, pp. 1–18, July 7, 1972.

Weinraub, Bernard, "Study Backs U.S. Nuclear Posture." New York Times, January 10, 1978.

"West Valley and the Nuclear Waste Dilemma." 12th Report by Committee on Government Operations together with Additions and Dissenting Views, October 26, 1977, Union Calendar No. 394, 95th Congress, 1st Session, Report No. 95–755.

Wilford, John Noble, "Radiation Tests Set for Bikini Islands." New York Times, March 23, 1978.

"World Armaments, The Nuclear Threat." Stockholm International Peace Research Institute, 1977.

Yergin, Daniel, "The Real Meaning of the Energy Crunch." The New York Times Magazine, June 4, 1978.